9/17
Am

FOR THE WORLD'S GREATEST KID,
WHO HAPPENS TO BE MINE.

Geezer Dad
by Tom LaMarr

Printed in the United States of America.
Published by Marcinson Press, Jacksonville, Florida
© Copyright 2015 by Tom LaMarr

Additional copies of this book may be purchased through
most online book retailers and by request through major
and independent bookstores. To purchase this book for
your library or in bulk, please contact the publisher at
www.marcinsonpress.com.

ISBN 978-0-9967207-0-0

Published by
Marcinson Press
10950-60 San Jose Blvd., Suite 136
Jacksonville, FL 32223 USA
http://www.marcinsonpress.com

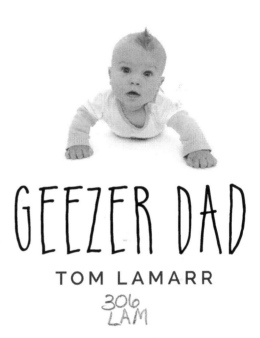

GEEZER DAD

TOM LAMARR

The only thing

constant in life is

change.
_____

HERACLITUS

CHAPTER ONE

GOOD NEWS. BAD NEWS.

If it wasn't the boldest decision anyone ever made, it was big for us. After years spent discussing, debating, and generally overthinking our options, we would stop trying to *not* have a baby. We would place our fate in nature's hands, enjoy some wine each night with dinner, and see if anything happened.

Something did. We were going to be parents.

We had put in our time as a childless couple. When I first met Sam in her home state of Florida, compact discs were a gimmick that would never take hold. In New York City, she accepted my proposal, hours after dining at Windows on the World, atop a 107-story building that no longer exists. The restaurants and museums of Washington, D.C., placed the world within walking distance of our first home, a slim, three-story townhouse. I started my own business as a freelance writer, and was encouraged to learn that my neighbor also worked at home — until I looked out one afternoon to see our street turned into a police-station parking lot. His crack house, apparently, had not been properly licensed. The barrels of semi-automatic rifles, dozens of them, gleamed in the sun.

Three years into our marriage, we moved to Colorado to be closer to family (my brother, an uncle, two aunts, and six cousins) as well as the Rockies (the mountains, not the baseball team). Sam went back to school and landed an ideal job in the field of renewable energy. I worked weekends and nights for clients who compensated me well for the inconvenience of being handcuffed to a computer, and as a result, we bought a more desirable house than I ever thought I'd see with an English degree. Although we had lost our proximity to the National Gallery of Art, the incidence of crack-house raids was greatly reduced. For the first time in our lives, Sam and I felt settled.

A modest commute northwest of Denver, our small suburb had not surrendered all of its character when stripped of its identity as a coal-mining town. Main Street still claimed a disproportionate number of authentic Italian restaurants, and a half-century-old fire burns to this day in one of the tunnels beneath Old Town. Our neighbors proved more interesting and diverse than the ones I'd been expecting to meet, and our bedroom windows opened to postcard views of the Continental Divide. It seemed like a good place to raise a kid.

Now in her second month of pregnancy, Sam had never been more radiant — or obsessed. She went cold turkey, bidding farewell to her two twelve-ounce bottles of Flying Dog beer with Friday night pizza. She made lists of baby names that wouldn't sound silly in five years. Our groceries were chosen with care; she added new colors like yellow and green.

We were being set up.

The miscarriage left us irreparably battered. We worked, read, ate, and slept as before, but we were not the same. "It feels like someone stole our lives and replaced them with habits," Sam said to me as I pulled out my Rent-One-Get-One-Free coupon. We were waiting in line at Videoglut, as we did every Thursday evening. (People still rented video tapes then.)

"You think our lives are a series of habits?" I said. "I don't know. Say, do you have four pennies? With tax, it always comes out to four dollars and twenty-nine cents."

Our house seemed bigger, emptier, quieter. Music didn't help. The walls absorbed all sound. Complicating matters, it soon became clear that the two of us weren't going through the same crisis. When Sam told me she was "grieving," I couldn't simply nod and say, "I know exactly what you're feeling." Having seen the fetal tissue — and having carried it in a clear plastic bag to the medical clinic, an experience I could have done without — I had difficulty perceiving it as a human being. What I had seen was a collection of cells, an unformed pink glob that couldn't have weighed three ounces, and had never been destined to become something greater. This wasn't the same as losing my dad. I felt pain, but for Sam alone, for the weight I couldn't help carry. Of course, I was able to understand that her mourning was for the concept, for the promise of a child. But I wasn't ready to bury that concept. "We know we can get pregnant," I said. "We weren't even off the pill that long. It can't be that hard to have a baby."

I was wrong — three words that appear frequently in this account.

What I did see clearly was a lover and friend in distress. The radiance had faded, leaving only obsession. Sam no longer felt ambivalent. She wanted a child. Preferably that instant.

"I've watched my friends get pregnant," she said. "Their kids are all they talk about." Although I recalled conversations with these same friends about books, music, politics, and weather, I understood why Sam's memory had become so selective. This was a woman with a profound maternal instinct. In her office and book club, she had always been the leader, the planner. She was the one who collected for birthdays and showers, the one who arrived at potluck dinners with food enough for everyone. Only one technicality prevented her from being Mom of the Year: her not having the child she was meant to nurture and cherish. "I want to hear someone say, 'Mommy, I love you.' To me. Is that too much to ask from life?"

Compounding our discomfort, I had prevailed a few weeks earlier in making the case: "What harm could there be in telling our families and a few close friends?" As a result, our misfortune stalked us. Moms and brothers called to offer support and see how we were doing. "You and Sam must really be grieving." We couldn't get away from what had gone wrong.

Penny and Carl, two thoughtful friends who happen to be neighbors and successful parents, showed up one evening with flowers, a gesture that brought needed color and cheer into our home. Their act of kindness made me look bad as well, given that they had selfishly written their own names on the card. I was the one who should have ordered flowers, and would have ordered flowers had I not forgotten how, thanks to our two surrogate children. House cats their entire lives, Bud and Hobbes love nothing more than having nature delivered to them in a vase, meaning a bouquet is generally good for a day after it shows up on our doorstep. The boys are partial to petals, leaves, and stems. The card is usually spared. If a flower arrangement is to have any chance of survival in this less-than-friendly environment, it must seek shelter, fast, on the floor of our shower, its beauty locked behind smoky glass, out of reach to man and cat.

As if saying, "I dare you two to mess with me now," Sam placed the vase on a dresser in our bedroom. But the boys seemed to know that these flowers were special, and left them alone for an extra ten hours. My wife savored the post-impressionistic splashes of pink, red, and blue right up until I heard her shout, "Damn it, Bud, get away from the flowers!" The exhibit closed that evening, with the janitor — me — vacuuming up the petals and stems, or what could be loosely identified as such.

Two other good friends, Ellen and Jane, came to our house with news and a book. The news? They had just submitted a sizable first payment to Global Chinese American Adoptions. They were going to be a family. The book they brought continued the theme. *The Lost Daughters of China*. A used copy. From the wonderfully funky used bookstore in Old Town, just off of Main Street. Ellen's the owner. "You should consider it," Jane said. "Read the book."

My wife told Jane that we'd do both, and I knew she would read the book. But I also knew Sam wanted two things no adoption agency could provide: the experience of pregnancy, and holding her own infant in her arms.

In addition to the book, chrysanthemums, and gerbera daisies, we received one piece of helpful information: Miscarriages are fairly common and often precede a healthy pregnancy. Many successful mothers, including my own, had suffered one or more along the way.

"Absolutely true," revealed Mom. "First time I was pregnant. You now have three brothers. Eddie, Mac, and that other one. You know, your father liked to say that all our pregnancies ended in disappointment."

I asked if she was joking; there was silence on the line. She was calling from Iowa. Many of our closest family members lived far away, mine in the Midwest, Sam's in Florida, Maryland,

and Tennessee. In the months that followed, Mom sent thousands of encouraging emails, like, "You'll have beautiful children!" and "I'm thinking of moving out there when it happens!"

Sam's dad, mom, and sister prayed for our success, and let us know they were doing so. Whenever they asked, "Anything new?"... we provided the silence. They soon figured out it was best not to ask.

Medical science came to our aid, forming an alliance that wouldn't always be so welcome. The fetal tissue found its way to a lab, and a nurse at our clinic took us aside to say what I'd been thinking: "These cells were never meant to develop further. Sometimes the genes just don't match up." This finding, unfortunately, marked the beginning of our long-term frustration. No one could ever tell us what was or was not working. Our chances looked good, words we would hear again and again.

There was one more problem, one that had already cost us valuable time. Though Sam was now ruled by that damn bio-clock, predictably ticking like a time bomb in a bad movie, I still felt pangs of ambivalence, particularly in restaurants where children ran from table to table reenacting the French and Indian War. Working at home, I had grown accustomed to long periods of solitude and quiet, and while denying I suffered from workaholism, I couldn't help but wonder how a child would cut into my twenty-six hour workday.

On a Friday night, just as I was warming to that week's movie rental, Sam calmly explained why a baby would be good for me: "You work all the time. You *are* a workaholic." She also reminded me that no two cats had ever known a more doting parent. "Stop thinking so much. You'll be a great dad."

"I know. I know." I tried to explain that I wasn't being obdurate — or insensitive. A kid would be great, and furthermore, I was cooperating to the best of my ability. "It will happen. We know that. I just don't see our marriage as a vacuum waiting to be filled. I like what we have." I could tell we were missing a critical scene. Had there been a way to covertly secure the remote, I would have paused the tape. "As lives go, these aren't bad ones."

"That's your head. Try bringing your heart into the process." Tears were forming, not a good sign. "You frustrate the hell out of me by stifling your emotions. This isn't supposed to be logical. Sometimes, I really feel like I'm on my own."

A friend suggested we get our feet wet, specifically by babysitting her infant. We babysat. The baby cried, and I could see that babies were like pets. Every pet owner loves his own "sweet poochiekins" while pitying his poor, stupid, cur-coddling neighbors for putting up with all the barking and soiled carpets. As I'd often heard, "Having your own is different," and my history supported this claim. I had never particularly wanted cats, until Sam dragged me out of the house one Saturday morning to a K-Mart parking lot in suburban Washington, where some cat-friendly volunteers were trying to find homes for an unfortunate menagerie of kitty orphans. We chose two, and they immediately realized that I was their First Class ticket to whatever they wanted, whenever they wanted. They spent the next months training me, and by the time they were through, I couldn't imagine a world without Bud and Hobbes. This was generally how I fell in love with new cities and continents. Sam would insist we needed a vacation, and after grudgingly accepting that I'd be sleepless and constipated for days — trapped in planes and strange hotel rooms, trying to plug electric razors into outlets that made no sense — I would rediscover just how good it felt to get away from my desk, and London or Sydney or Akumal would quickly get the better of my poor judgment.

One good night's sleep and tourists on the Underground were asking me for directions.

Since Sam had been right about kittens and travel, it stood to reason that her instincts were right about starting a family. I also understood that the rut I cherished wouldn't always be so comfortable — that the things I viewed as constant would change and even vanish. Friends would move away or worse, and I knew it unlikely that our cats would be jumping onto my desk in fifteen years' time to show me the "A"'s they had earned on their undergraduate theses. (Bud had already expressed reservations about continuing his education beyond high school.) Children, I gathered, came with longer life expectancies. You could also presumably train them to do things, like mow the lawn and vacuum up flowers, tasks the cats had trouble with.

While a few friends asked, "Why is it you want to wake up to screams and green diapers?" most assured me I'd be a natural father. They told me I possessed great reserves of patience I had somehow failed to notice on my own and that I had much to teach another human being. "Look, you dumb ass, the only way to appreciate parenthood is to experience it. What if you'd never tried food? Or sex? Or food with sex?" Once again, I knew they were right. I'd do fine as a dad, and I'd enjoy the experience, much as I enjoyed food and sex.

Ellen brought up a larger point: "You're afraid it will hurt your writing."

I was sitting on the bench in her bookstore, which everyone in town used as a psychiatrist's couch. "Free therapy," she liked to say. "And worth every penny." Ellen knew everything about everyone: who was getting divorced, who should have been getting divorced, who needed to refine their shoplifting skills, and who was addicted to romance novels.

"You're right," I said. "It's not that I fear becoming a stay-at-home dad. It's that I won't find time to write." My first novel was trudging toward publication at the time, and while I took pride in finally sitting myself down and doing one thing properly, I didn't expect the book to make me independently wealthy — or even pay for a nanny. (Raising the stakes, one of my larger freelance clients had elected to become a pain in the wallet area, making it clear that younger, more desperate English majors would give up their weekends for less. Issuing their edict from a Central Office, based I believe, in southeastern Mordor, these particular advertising overlords had come up with a "more consistent fee scale" to bring my prices in line. I, in turn, decided to stop groveling, and Sam supported that decision. "You can afford to give up one client," she said the evening their new subsistence-wage scale showed up on our fax, "and concentrate more on your fiction. Look at the responses you're getting. You've got to see how it plays out. No one ever whispered on their deathbed, 'I wish I'd written more advertising.'")

"Look," Ellen said now as she sorted through a stack of beat-up paperback thrillers. "You know three things. You want to be a dad. You want Sam to be happy. And you want to write more books. You're afraid you'll settle for two out of three. But let's consider something else." She took a sip of coffee. "I can see how a child would make you a better writer."

I listened closely. Ellen had earned acclaim as a painter, had scored her own shows in Denver and Boulder. I trusted her opinion. "Experience," she said. "Isn't that a good thing?"

"I've thought about that," I said. "It's just— I don't want to be one of those parents who blames his family for keeping him from some impossible goal. You know the ones. They're out on our cul-de-sac every Saturday morning teaching their eight-month-olds to play hockey."

"Trust yourself. You love what you do and you've got discipline that bears an eerie resemblance to obsession. My honest opinion? Triplets couldn't mess you up at this point."

"You don't think Sam and I could—"

"Wait till you're sixty? No, I don't think so."

"I'll have to give up sleep," I said. "There's not enough time as it is."

Ellen could have asked where the heck I found time to come to her store and grumble, but she chose to be kind, saying, "You'll have to do that anyway. It's part of being a parent."

Pricing a copy of *Commie Sub Commander*, she continued, "Maybe you're fortunate." She pointed the book at my chest. "Most people I meet are just killing time. They have much more of it than they have interests. How else do you explain malls? Or TV awards shows? Hell, look at most of the books I sell. You know, if you ever decided to become an optimist, you'd soon realize that the old you worried too much."

"You think I worry too much?"

"I think you should get back to work and make a few bucks to pay for all the things your baby will need. Motivation. It's also a good thing."

Walking home, I saw that Ellen was right, except for the part about triplets. That would mess me up. But a cathartic experience that opened my eyes, mind, and heart probably wouldn't hurt my writing.

And so I stood firmly by Plan A: a little wine, some Marvin Gaye... and whatever happened, happened.

Sam, however, had progressed several plans into the alphabet. She was marking up calendars and bringing home books. She kept buying those green things we had stumbled upon in the produce aisle.

Early one Tuesday while looking for a sweater without cat hair on it, she said, "The baby. We need to try harder."

I told her I was available most nights.

"Nights aren't enough," she replied.

Naively, I thought, *Hmm, I'm going to have lots of sex. This won't be bad.* The possibility that there was such a thing as too much sex, that a man could end up wanting to stage an accident — Sorry, babe, cut off my penis while sharpening the lawn mower blades; can't have sex today — never once entered my mind.

"Do you want a child?" she asked. "It's a simple question. Yes or no?"

"Yes," I told her. "I do."

At last, we were in agreement. We were going to try harder. No more ambivalence, no more waiting.

One of the appointments Sam had marked on a calendar would cause us regret — and help make it necessary for me to use reading glasses when measuring formula. Our doctor, a physician we greatly trusted and respected, had called, wanting to discuss the miscarriage. "Could you come in on Wednesday?" No problem, we thought. He can share some medical tricks on ensuring a successful pregnancy.

He had other plans for us.

The question that is so

clearly in many potential

parents' minds:

Why should we stunt our

ambitions and impoverish

our lives in order to be

insulted and looked down

upon in our old age?

———————————

JOSEPH SCHUMPETER

CHAPTER TWO
ANTI—SEX AIDS.

"Getting pregnant on the rebound is risky."

Dr. Bedlow adjusted his glasses and continued, "I strongly suggest you hold off a few months. It's clear you're both fertile and that time isn't an issue." Steady and sure, his words took the form of friendly advice. As we knew from our visits as individual patients, he wasn't the kind of doctor who talked down to people like me whose diplomas weren't worth framing. I'd always felt at ease when he appraised my moles. Now he was saying, "Another pregnancy so soon could be emotionally harmful."

We didn't think to ask, "Risky? Harmful? Could you show us the thousand-page study?"

"I'll see you again in three months," he said. "Until then, birth control. Prophylactics are fine. Until you figure out exactly what you're feeling."

This struck us as odd. But again, we liked Dr. Bedlow, and trusted Dr. Bedlow. He seemed a good listener; perhaps he had sensed a lingering trace of ambivalence.

By the time Sam and I figured out that we already knew what

we were feeling — and that prophylactics weren't especially fine — we had also figured out our doctor. Adam Bedlow, we saw with painful clarity, was a family-practice physician who got all the family he needed at work. He was firmly, if secretly in the "Why would any rational adult want to have children?" camp.

Returning to his office for our three-month follow-up, I couldn't believe how many clues we'd missed, because the damn things were everywhere — specifically, in his choice of photos. True, there was one of his spouse on a calendar advertising her real-estate gig. But the remaining portraits kept Bedlow connected to a family of Chevy Corvettes. Red, blue, and silver, these were his children, undemanding, undented — and unlikely to spit up on the good doctor's cashmere sweater.

"Have you reached any conclusions?" he asked, and we shared our thoughts on grief, hope, and kids.

"We want a family," said Sam. "We know that."

"Then it's clear to me you're ready."

Sam held back her frustration, saving it for the drive home in our non-Corvette. "I hereby pronounce you ready," she mimicked, fidgeting with a pair of invisible glasses. For the time being, Bedlow wouldn't pay the price for tossing away three perfectly good reproductive cycles. No, that would be us. Sam and me.

For the next several months we tried killing our sex life at home, alone, without the professional assistance that would come later. We scheduled our intercourse — the word lovemaking no longer applied — so that it coincided with her peak ovulation. The result was Mussolini sex, getting those trains into the station on time with no thought for joy, desire, or human frailty. No sooner had the last passenger disembarked from The 9:15 Outbound than Sam pushed me aside and twisted herself into positions that showed more respect for gravity than basic comfort or the visuals burning themselves into her husband's long-term memory.

Outside of the bedroom, she popped vitamins by the handful, made me do the same. She exercised and read articles on "How to Get the Most from Sex," with the "most" referring to something besides pleasure. She brought home kits that measured her readiness. And she wept quietly, thinking I didn't see, each time menstruation began.

When Dr. Bedlow called us back in we felt older and, for the first time, desperate. Eight months had passed since the miscarriage.

"Uh-hm," he said, glancing at something inside a folder, "maybe you're not so fertile." The lightness of his tone produced the opposite of its intended effect. Though he didn't seem to notice, Sam was buckling under the weight of his indifference. "I could refer you to a specialist, help you get the most buck for your bang."

While I wondered, Did he really just say that? Sam leaned forward in her chair. "Does he specialize in time travel?" she asked, an icy anger in her voice. "Because that's what we need at this point—" She had already alerted me on the drive to his office that she wanted to change primary-care physicians, but had left out the part about strangling Bedlow to put this into motion. There in his office, she finished her thought: "As opposed to say, prophylactics."

His glasses came all the way off. "What do you mean?"

"We've lost valuable time."

"Ah, the miscarriage—"

"Why did you make us wait? I want to have a baby. There's never been any question of that."

"It is true you can only spoil your pets so much."

My wife seemed ready to cry (and again, to strangle a health-care professional). "This is important to us, Dr. Bedlow. Why can't you see that?"

The glasses went back on. "I wouldn't rule out a positive outcome just yet. You have plenty of options. And I'm recommending a specialist who knows these much more intimately than I do." He was writing as he spoke. "I'm sorry about the delay," he continued, handing Sam a referral slip. "I really am. Sometimes we make mistakes."

"And why did you take three months off?" asked Dr. Moody. "You're hardly at an age where you have fertility to burn. The doctors who say you have till you're forty are wrong. The studies I've read show dramatic changes occurring throughout a woman's thirties. Provided she hasn't previously conceived."

The specialist looked small behind an imposing redwood desk, its workspace strangely barren save for a pair of eight-by-ten photos, framed in dark silver and facing outward so that patients could admire them without straining their necks. In sharp contrast to Bedlow's Corvettes, the first introduced an infant daughter, her bald head topped with a massive pink bow that kept patients from asking, "And how old is he?" In the other formal portrait, physician and spouse stood side by side behind a frilly bassinet, admiring that child and her bow.

I thought of my own office desk, its surface utterly lost beneath clippings and notes, dozens of strata. Photos didn't stand a chance in that clutter.

"Still," Dr. Moody said, "Your chances look good. You've been pregnant once. And you both seem to be in pretty good health." The clinic would run a few tests "to make sure everything's where it's supposed to be." In the meantime, she wrote our first prescription.

Clomid – though taken only several days each month – would lubricate Sam's ovaries and increase the production of eggs. There were possible side effects.

"Like in those commercials aimed at hypochondriacs?" I asked.

"Exactly," Moody said with a smirk. "Don't forget to ask your doctor about Happytrin."

"So what are they?" Sam said sternly, a Kindergarten teacher breaking up horseplay. "The side effects?"

"The worst," she replied, "is mild depression. I know what you're thinking — just what the doctor ordered. As if you need pills to bring you down with what you've been through."

But not to worry, she added. Hot flashes were far more prevalent.

"A patient in northern Minnesota slept with her windows open in February." She got up from her chair. "Yours won't be that bad. Questions?"

"Just one," I said. "Do you have samples of Happytrin?"

We scheduled our tests with her nurse. Sam agreed to return a few days later, while I had to "bring something in" after going three days without sexual gratification of any sort. The nurse told me to keep my sample warm. She advised me to carry it next to my skin. I would have thirty minutes to make the drop.

She handed me a plastic vial with a black screw-on cap.

Though relieved to know it went into a container before hitching a ride beneath my shirt, I still had one concern. What if I was in an accident? What would they think at State Farm?

"You should probably avoid accidents. Remember, you've only got half an hour."

She returned her attention to a computer screen as Sam grabbed my sleeve and pulled me toward the exit.

"I like Dr. Moody," she said in the car. "I think she can help us."

I liked her, too. But I couldn't help but think we had signed away our lives, the ones that fit comfortably like well-worn bedroom slippers. This thought made me mildly depressed.

There was only one thing for me to do. I visited Ellen's bookstore late the next morning.

"How are you holding up?" a voice greeted me from the Sci-Fi room.

"Like Sisyphus," I said.

"Rolling the rock uphill?"

"Hardest worker in Hell."

She emerged from Sci-Fi and gave me a hug. "I hear it's really hot this time of year."

"Not as bad as you'd expect," I replied, taking my seat on the bench. "I'm still working on faith that I'll reach the summit. Until then, all I can do is keep pushing, and keep telling myself it's good exercise. But Sam. I didn't expect to see her so beat up and bruised. I'd like to see her smile again."

"If it hadn't been for the miscarriage—"

"She'd be a new mom right now."

"Want to grab some lunch?" Ellen asked.

I suggested the Happy Wok. Half a block away, their carryout was fast, and their fortune cookies always came through with guarantees of fabulous wealth. "Everyone's a winner," I promised Ellen. "None of this *people respect you for your honesty* crap."

"Yeah," she said, "who needs that?"

Minutes later, she was poking at her Ma-Pau tofu medley with chopsticks. I was back on the bench.

"You saw the new doctor?"

"We're about to be examined, inside and out."

"An alien abduction," she offered, "complete with probes."

Another of Ellen's regulars came into the store. A stout, older woman, she looked at the bench and frowned profusely, making it clear she was disappointed to find it in use. "Hey, Florence," Ellen said. "You're in early." The woman simply grunted. I'd seen this before — the bookstore as talk show. Ellen was David Letterman, of course, and Florence the guest who had just been bumped.

The woman hovered close, listening in. She probably didn't know she was pretending to look for titles in the Improving Intimacy section.

"Sam's getting the worst of it," I told Ellen. "But that doesn't mean I'm yearning to be scrutinized. What if they say, 'We take it you tried LSD a time or two'? No one will care if it was 5,000 years ago. I don't want to be singled out as the cause of our problem."

"You'd think five millennia would place you outside the statute of limitations."

I dipped my egg roll in mustard, took a bite, and uttered four syllables that caused Florence to glare at me with even more hostility. "Sorry," I wheezed. "This mustard's laced with kerosene."

Ellen laughed. "You'll have to stop talking like that when baby shows up, you realize. That's the current project at our house. Washing our vocabularies out with soap."

"The sacrifices never stop," I said. "How do people do it?" The burning subsided, a forest fire that had run out of trees, or in this case, undamaged nerve endings. "Say, Ellen. I know you tried acid when you were young. You ever worry about your chromosomes?"

"Hell, no," she said, smiling slyly. "One more advantage to adopting."

She lowered her spring roll into a syrupy brown concoction that, going by her lack of reaction, was not injurious to organs or tissue. "They won't find anything wrong with your chromosomes," she said.

"You're probably right," I conceded. "They're just going to tell us to bathe in frigid saltwater and sleep on concrete blocks and only have sex while hanging upside down in elevator shafts and chanting."

My sinuses were draining — completely. I reached into the brown paper bag our food had come in, hoping to find fresh napkins to dam my nostrils. "I think we kept trying on our own for as long as we did because we didn't want to consider the next step. But here we are."

Florence chose that moment to storm off the talk-show set, giving the door a hard pull for emphasis. "She probably wanted to dump on her nephew," Ellen said. "She's terrified he's gay. Old Florence is not my most observant customer."

My friend made out like a CEO when it came time to divide the fortune cookies. *You will be one of the richest members of your generation*, hers revealed.

I would have been happier for Ellen had the Wok not failed me for the first time ever. "What's happening to the world I know?" I asked after snapping my cookie in half. "*Your tenacity is a virtue*? Geez, Ellen, you're cashing out your retirees' pension fund, and all I get is a generic food-court fortune."

"Upward mobility isn't for everyone," she said. "Want to buy a bookstore?"

———————————————————

Monday, Dr. Moody called to exonerate me. "All systems are go," she said. "I don't think it's unrealistic to expect a pregnancy at some point. Worst case scenario — other aids are available."

"Then why aren't we pregnant?" Sam asked when I phoned her at work. "Why hasn't it happened?"

I didn't remind her it happened once. She told me she needed to stop at the drug store. To pick up new fertility kits.

"Remember when it was candles and wine? A rental copy of *Red Shoe Diaries*?"

"Vaguely," she said, and I watched helplessly as our past broke away, a massive chunk of ice splitting off from a berg.

Sam surprised me that evening, however, showing up with an Australian Chardonnay and a rented movie – *Dangerous Liaisons*. "Hmm, Michelle Pfeiffer and Uma Thurman," I said.

"And John Malkovich," she quickly pointed out. "This isn't one of our do-or-die-trying nights."

A second pleasant surprise made itself known over the next few weeks. The Clomid did not cause depression. Sam experienced a few hot flashes, but didn't once pull out *The Essential Bessie Smith*, find "Nobody Knows You When You're Down and Out," and push the Repeat-This-Track-Till-The-Cows-Come -Home button.

As for our quest, it was business as usual. Perfunctory Liaisons. Like good little fascists, we adhered to our practice of Mussolini sex, the timing still dictated by sticks that changed color when treated disrespectfully. The instant we finished, I did worse than change color, becoming invisible, while Sam, aided by pillows doing things pillows weren't designed to do, strained to perfect her post-coital contortionist act for Cirque du Soleil.

Unfortunately, however, the Clomid also failed to deliver that one big effect we desired. The fertility test strips changed color; the pregnancy ones did not.

Sam saw Dr. Moody on a monthly basis, and as these visits piled up, they proved every bit as dispiriting as the other monthly ones. One year in, we vacationed in the Bahamas to take our minds off the fact that time had sided against us... and to see if exotic locations would improve our obsessively procreative sex. At the fifteen-month mark we bought a home theater system with 5.1 surround.

When the doctor asked Sam to bring me along for Visit Seventeen, we knew it couldn't be good. "If Clomid's going to work on its own," Doc Moody said, "it should've happened by now. I think we need to explore new options."

And so our specialist gave us the name of another specialist. "Dr. Webb. Just down the hill in Boulder. He's known as a master at working off the biological clock.

"I'm sorry," she continued. "I truly was hoping I'd be one of the first to share in your good news."

"I need to warn you that one thing changes from here on out," Dr. Webb began. "In some states, insurers are required by law to view infertility as just one more medical condition. Colorado isn't one of those states."

He could have added, "But don't despair. We accept three kinds of coverage. Visa, MasterCard, and home equity loans." As we were about to learn, our time with Dr. Moody had been golden in one respect, in that our HMO had covered the visits. True, they had charged a hefty co-pay and challenged each claim a minimum of two times, with Sam making phone calls from her office to their Cancel Every Claim Until Repeatedly Challenged Department. But they always paid up in the end, however grudgingly.

Dr. Webb suggested we try artificial insemination. A positive outcome was a statistical probability, he said, given that Sam was not yet forty and that we'd been pregnant once. "Two consecutive mornings each month. Until we get that fat lady singing."

"A statistical probability?" Sam asked.

"If you're willing to pursue this wholeheartedly. And there are other options. It's a brave new world inside these doors."

Sam told Webb to sign us up. I wanted to ask if he'd ever read Huxley's novel.

It didn't matter. We were about to take up residence in its pages. Since the miscarriage, Sam and I had succeeded in removing the pleasure from sex. Now, with Dr. Webb's help, we were about to eliminate that bothersome sex altogether.

Man is the only animal that

blushes – or needs to.

———————————————

MARK TWAIN

CHAPTER THREE

THE THINGS WE DO FOR LOVE.

Yes, I have debased myself in doctor's offices. But discarding a few moments here and there, it wasn't much fun and was never destined to become a fetish. I'm saying this up front because it's the most embarrassing thing in this chapter and possibly the book. Now, we can all take a deep breath and proceed (though I sincerely request you forget this chapter the moment you finish reading).

For those lacking firsthand knowledge of artificial insemination, it's survival of the fittest in microcosm. It's also where the middleman comes into the process. Prospective dads agreeing to this option entrust their semen to licensed health care professionals who place it in a variety of plasticware while washing it off, then toss it in the medical equivalent of a blender until the hardiest little swimmers rise to the top. "Keep paddling, Robert. For Pete's sake, keep paddling." This proud new race of supersperm is then inserted (in lay terms, squirted) deep into the appropriate vagina. The insertion-specialist-nurse employs a long, thin plastic tube to achieve this final goal. She's aided, too, by metal torture devices that women apparently know from their visits to gynecologists, and that — for reasons unclear to me — have been stored on ice the night before. The nurse feigns ignorance — "I'm sorry. Is that cold?" — but I think she's enjoying this. "Oh dear, it is uncomfortable, isn't it?" Forget champagne. Forget flowers. This is romance, the kind one finds only in a doctor's office with harsh fluorescent lighting — or sleeping on an in-law's foldout couch.

The first part of this process is tricky, of course, because as any man reading this knows, coming up with the goods is somewhat more complicated than saying, "Sperm? Sure, just happen to have some. And there's plenty more where that came from." Frankly, I haven't been able to say this since I was seventeen and lying awake at night hosting impure thoughts about the airbrushed "supermodel" on the poster on my wall. These days, instant gratification takes forever, though my wife assures me this is a good thing. Not so at the fertility clinic, where no one has ever whispered, "Slow down, babe. Make it last."

The digital clock-radio might have been placed in the Donor Room to give nervous patients the option of soothing their savage beasts with music — "You're grooving with Kenny G on EZ-105" — but I suspected its main purpose is to remind 7:30 Donor that 7:45 Donor was also paying good money for the privilege of using that room. As I quickly learned, artificial insemination requires a fair amount of manual participation — not to mention a level of concentration I always managed to leave at home — and I felt under the gun to produce. I didn't need to hear someone pounding on the door. "Hey, pal, there's a line out here. Give the rest of us a chance."

The funniest thing about artificial insemination is that sex is prohibited for three days beforehand. It's important to build that sperm count, and heaven forbid I impregnate my wife without others looking on. Not so amusing are the cost and humiliation — two factors that helped make our first visit that much more memorable.

The morning started with a twenty-minute drive to a doctors' complex, taking separate cars so that Sam could continue on to work, where she would squirm in the same chair for eight hours straight, ignoring complaints from her stomach and bladder, while pressing her thighs together to ensure that nothing snuck back out. "Hold on, Robert! You've traveled too far to give in now. Swim toward the light. Swim toward the light." Here's how I recall that inaugural visit, conceding that my memory is helped by the fact we returned many times.

The receptionist seems pleasant enough for 7:30 in the morning. "Cash up front," she says calmly, "credit cards welcome." It hits me that this the closest I've ever come to paying for sex, though I'm willing to bet I'd get a lot more service in a Nevada brothel for the amount she's putting on that card. She wants to see my insurance card too, and while I oblige, I already know our HMO won't chip in because they treat this as if it were prostitution. I find this ironic, since they're the ones who always leave us feeling screwed.

Once my cards are back in my wallet and I've signed away the equivalent of a Cambodian teacher's annual wages, a nurse appears in a doorway. She invites me to "Come this way, Tom," and leads me to a dimly lit room, small for an office, spacious for a Men's room. Furnished with couch, cabinet, and yes, sink and toilet, this is the Donor Room. She stops shy of the door — so much for her willingness to help, as well as the shameful state of healthcare in the United States. The door closes and I must try to remember why we're doing this, I must think of "the baby." But the idea of new life seems as alien to this place as pro bono clients. The walls are spare, no

Sears Family Portraits of wide-eyed, smiling toddlers, no wall-paper-trim depictions of hippos and hamsters and sidewinder snakes queuing to board an ark.

Blinds hide a window on the opposite wall. These probably open to the street; I figure I'll keep them closed. Next, I'm looking under the couch and prying open cabinet doors until I find a stack of *Playboys* and something called *Perfect 10*, cringing at the thought that these magazines have been touched by hundreds of other men wearing their underwear down around their ankles. At least there's soap and water in a dispenser above the sink, and as I proceed to Step Two — underwear in place — I am further aroused by the sounds of professional health care technicians going about their business.

Oh, please, nursey, please, I want to shout. *You dirty, dirty girl. Could you repeat those words, 'Do we have a sperm count for Mr. Smith?'* I must concentrate... concentrate... and stop glancing at the stupid digital clock. *Go away, Mr. Smith. Get out of my fantasy. Just try to focus on the task at hand. Ah, that's better... better... better. 'Oh yes, Miss November, will you mother my child?'*

Finally, the cap goes on the plastic vial, at which time I'm grateful to have already jotted my last name on an adhesive label that will grace the container. With pride and shaky penmanship, I do add one last piece of information, writing 100 on the "percent of emission" line.

More good news: No one's pounding on the door. But this doesn't mean I'm in the clear. I must deposit my deposit in an in-box conveniently located on the middle of a wide, bright counter near the front desk (I'm waiting for a bell or siren to sound) and crawl back into the waiting room, avoiding the eyes of lesbian couples who are clearly thinking, *Jeez, I hope they don't give us his sperm.*

Once in the seat Sam's been saving for me, I try to read the morning paper, hoping I won't find headlines on the order of, "Childless Colorado Author Masturbates in Doctor's Office." Concentrate... concentrate. Now here's a human-interest story to hold my attention — and to remind me I must make that appointment to upgrade my prescription reading glasses: "Playboy's Miss November Admits She Used to Be a Man." This is when my wife takes my hand — the other one — and calms me by saying, "Honey, where did you leave your pants?"

I won't see my sperm for another hour, and some of it, sadly, is lost to me forever. But for my adventurous seed, it's an eventful sixty minutes, basically the sperm equivalent of those "reality" game shows created by visionaries at Fox and CBS to avoid paying writers and actors (and to convince terrorist organizations that our culture really isn't worth attacking). "Tonight on Survival Down Under, find out which unlucky spermatozoon gets voted off the tube? The viewer decides the outcome, something you can't say for The Sopranos or West Wing — or for that matter, books. Eight o'clock. Seven central."

Sam and I spend most of the hour in relative calm, fidgeting, reading, and trying not to peek at the other infertile couples that enter and exit the clinic. After forty minutes, we're escorted to a room that looks like a real doctor's office. It smells like one too, alcohol-clean, gamete-free. The nurse stays with us, no freezing up at the door this time. I ask about the expensive-looking machine that takes up a third of the room. "It's an ultrasound device," she explains, leaving off the words, "that you two will be paying for."

She lifts a phallic cylinder that's attached to the machine by way of vacuum cleaner hose. But the image the nurse wishes to maintain is the phallic one, so she places something that looks a lot like a prophylactic over the cylinder's head (Where was this mental image when I was stuck in that other room?) and lubricates it with a Vaseline-like gel. Gleaming in the room's bright lighting — here the overhead lights burn like the sun, the sun as seen from Mercury — this attachment shows no desire to erase old stereotypes. It behaves as expected, promptly making its way to my wife's most private parts. But here's a surprise. This phallus does one thing mine cannot — it takes pictures — and soon, we're looking at scenes from inside the womb on a twenty-inch screen similar to a computer's monitor. These images require some imagination on my part; they're murky and gray and could well be shots of caverns from a PBS nature special. "We are careful not to disturb the nesting vampire bats. Oh darn. We have disturbed the nesting vampire bats."

The nurse tells us that she's spotted an egg. "Looking good. Ooh, there's a second one in the left ovary. Excellent. Excellent." For my wife, hearing these kind words may be the only pleasure she gets in return for her trio of sex-free days. But I don't think it does much for her. She's never been vain about her eggs. Besides, she's about to learn that our nurse is free and easy with compliments. When the sperm make their entrance, already assembled in their slim plastic tube, the nurse beams. "This is excellent, Mr. LaMarr. The motility is excellent. We're looking good."

The count is something like 87 trillion, give or take a few zeroes, meaning that my wife would have to produce several more eggs to make this a fair contest. "It's looking great," the nurse exclaims, her pitch rising. "An excellent sample." It's my turn now to feel uneasy. After decades of waiting for someone to tell me I'm good at something, I'm disappointed to learn it's masturbation.

"Not all sperm are created equal," the nurse adds. "Our process weeds out the weaker specimens." She seems proud of her role in this Darwinian death match. "Plus, semen only live three days. Our aim is to achieve a younger, more vital population."

I am pleased to discover that the final step is not so cold and mechanical. (Well, actually it is cold, thanks to that freeze-dried gadget.) Sam and I hold hands and I press the trigger that completes the ancient insemination ritual. "Slow down, Mr. LaMarr," the nurse whispers. "Make it last." Smiling, she turns out the lights and leaves the room. She must also have pressed a button on this room's clock-radio, because an announcer is saying, "You're listening to the Big EZ and we're grooving with Kenny G."

"Thanks for doing this," Sam says. "You know it's important to me."

Heading home, I feel empty and weak, and I'm reminded of driving back to my apartment when I was in my twenties and dates sometimes stretched into wee morning hours. Since I'm reliving those memories, there's only one thing for me to do: stop and get fast food. A biscuit sounds good.

"I know that wasn't pleasant for either of us," Sam said when the first month's results came up negative. "It sure wasn't sexy. But you heard them. It's going to happen. It's got to."

"I feel I've set foot on a much surer path to humility than joining a Tibetan monastery," I said. "I want to turn back, but you're right. This is important." I didn't tell Sam what I had seen that day at Ellen's bookstore — a photo of the child who was waiting in China to meet her new family. Ellen had never been happier.

"This fertility stuff sounds like self-inflicted pain," Ellen had said. "Have you read *Lost Daughters of China* yet?"

Subsequent visits to the clinic varied little from the first, though I did have new reading glasses. "Fool me once, Miss

November, shame on you. Fool me twice..." Also, whenever Sam's cycles necessitated a weekend visit (I did mention this was all based on her cycles, didn't I?), the Boulder clinic was closed, forcing us to drive an additional hour to the opposite end of the metro area. On one such trek I earned my first photo-radar ticket, along with the page eight headline, "Childless Colorado Author Gets Ticket on Way to Masturbate in Doctor's Office."

"It could've been worse," a friend explained a few years later. "It could've been much, much worse." Steve had just become an adoptive dad, and I had just learned that he too was a fertility clinic veteran. During his first visit, he disclosed, he pried open the cabinet doors only to find a selection of medical publications. No doubt humming *The Things We Do for Love*[1] to himself, Steve chose to soldier on. For him, unfortunately, this did turn into a fetish, and to this day his wife is perplexed by his subscription to the *Journal of the American Medical Association*. Steve works in advertising. Non-medical clients. "Steve, honey, it's bedtime. You're straining your eyes with all that reading. It's been half an hour. There's a line out here. Give the rest of us a chance."

---

1 *Lordy, Lord, my book has a footnote. For those with fading memories, "The Things We Do for Love" was a hit for 10cc in the mid-seventies. Coincidentally – and this was only according to my friend Joe at the time – the band named itself for the metric volume of an average male ejaculation.*

CHAPTER FOUR

RECORD LOWS.

If the winter of our discontent showed any sign of easing it was only to taunt us. Sam and I were pregnant — twice. But each of these pregnancies lasted only weeks and might not have been detected had it not been for the steady surveillance of test kits and ultrasound.

The first, surprisingly, began without professional assistance. We had just scheduled our monthly appointment at the clinic, the timing determined by a fertility test kit. As the second purple stripe made clear, Sam was ovulating and would peak in three days, until which time it was my husbandly duty to save up sperm. But the flesh was weak and our spirits weaker, and in violation of the no-sex-involving-physical-contact rule, we gave in to desire. At home. In bed. As I recall, it felt pretty good.

We, of course, had no way of knowing we'd succeeded on our own, and thus still paid $700 to make sure our dehumanization efforts stayed current. "Your count's lower than usual," the nurse said in regard to my sample, "but everything's looking good. Quite good."

By the end of that week, we knew exactly how good, thanks

to Sam's newly cultivated habit of popping out pregnancy test kits whenever she had a hunch she might like the results... or a joint in her little finger ached... or one of the cats looked at her funny. For the first time in nearly three years, the strip changed color.

This landed us back in Webb's clinic, with Sam taking the morning off for her first "pre-natal" ultrasound. "Right there," the nurse said. "That's what we want to see. You're absolutely right, though. It does seem a little early." Orlandra, the nurse we'd seen most often, seemed genuinely happy for us. Or perhaps she was thinking, Finally. I won't have to look at these poor slobs every month.

Making the visit even more surreal, Webb's receptionist told me to put away the credit card... "well, except for the co-pay." Our insurance would cover these visits. "Now that you're pregnant."

Sam and I didn't talk much after we got home. Guardedly optimistic, or maybe just guarded, we knew better than to celebrate our news. Or share it with friends. Or say it out loud. We wouldn't be comparing lists of names for babies.

On Sunday we had brunch with Ellen and Jane, now a pair of beaming moms. Their daughter, Grace, was beautiful, greeting us with wide, inquisitive eyes that stole attention from her shimmering dark hair. All other eyes in the Happy Wok were checking her out.

"This," said Ellen as we made a second pass through the buffet line, "was meant to be."

When Jane added, "I still say you should look at adoption," we nodded politely and kept our secret.

This time, our fortune cookies distributed the wealth more evenly. Ellen and Jane were robber barons. I owned a string of five-star casinos. Sam alone came up short. *You will be taking a long trip*, hers revealed. But because she loved travel, and because she probably assumed I'd share some of my windfall with her, she seemed happy as a wok.

Four days later we were back in Webb's clinic and Orlandra was no longer smiling. She pointed to a bright spot on the ultrasound screen. "This... I'm sorry... we're not seeing any growth."

The doctor called us into his office. "Unfortunately—" We waited as Webb cleared his throat. "It's not a viable pregnancy. You can expect to miscarry within days." He then expressed his preference for accelerated grieving: "I know this is difficult. We can't blow this out of proportion, however. I still think it's encouraging that you can get pregnant."

Sam didn't speak. Nor did she cry — a detail I found troubling. When the session was over, she hopped in her car and pointed it south in the direction of her office, presumably thinking she might as well be miserable with pay, behind a hardwood door. I bought flowers on my way home.

Four months passed. Another strip changed color, proving at last that artificial insemination could result in something besides a hefty Visa balance. But when Sam miscarried — predicted again by ultrasound — I realized just how wary I'd become of the micromanagement that let us know each development, whether good or bad, the instant it happened. It was like having CNN mistake our most private struggle for a celebrity facing trial for criminal charges.

When Webb requested that we "come in for a talk," I knew what to expect. *Sure it's disheartening. But it would be wrong to quit now.* He wasn't going to lose his best clients. *Did Orlandra talk to you about membership in our Executive Club?* I imagined a ribbon-cutting ceremony five years into the future: "And of course, the LaMarr Wing of our new facility would not have been possible without..."

Since I was already fantasizing, I entertained a less likely scenario, that of Webb coming clean. "Sam, Tom," he would say as we took our seats on his couch and he closed the door in a rare nod to privacy. "It's our consensus that whatever the heck is encoded in your DNA can't be that vital to our species' survival. Why don't you two hold onto your hard-earned money, maybe take a nice vacation?"

This didn't happen.

In the clinic's waiting room, we met an actual flesh-and-blood mom. She played with her baby, laughed and smiled... and told us she was back for a sibling. "It worked for us," she said. "You've got to keep trying."

I knew a plant when I saw one.

"Your son is adorable," Sam told her as Webb appeared and motioned us into his office.

"We can't deny that the past days have been discouraging," he said, taking his seat behind the desk. "Yet I remain hopeful."

Webb paused for effect, his brow heavy with compassion. "You didn't by any chance meet Lynn in the waiting room? That poor woman endured four failed pregnancies. The Whites nearly gave up. Did she tell you that?" A sympathetic smile. "I tell you, I've seen it before. It's why I believe that artificial insemination will ultimately work for you."

But he seemed less convinced than before. I waited for him to unveil a statistic, a muscular number between 80 and 100 to buttress his "hopeful" claim. Without that support, he had nothing, zero.

As it turned out, none of this mattered, because even if Dr. Webb had bothered to dip into his vast reserve of numerical data, it would have been no match for a fortune cookie —

specifically, the fortune cookie Sam had received at the Happy Wok buffet. As you may recall, she had been promised a long trip, and sure enough, we were about to take one.

For eight tense, humid weeks in eastern Tennessee, the hours limped by like dogs hit by cars. Sam's mother was dying. Her cancer had not been in remission as we had been led to believe.

It started with a call from my father-in-law. When Luther found himself unable to speak, a visiting nurse took over. "April could go tonight," she said. "There's a serious risk of blockage."

That news had come on Saturday morning. By nightfall we lived in Sullivan County, just outside of Bristol.

Here was a world where two packs a day earned one the label of moderate smoker. And in a one-story, one-bathroom house choking on guests and secondhand tar, we dreamed, ate, and wore April's cancer. "It's no wonder she's sick," Sam said to me one night. "I'd give anything if Daddy would quit."

"As much as I love him," I agreed, "he's as bad as the rest of us at missing obvious signs." But I could have told her why he'd never stop. I had seen Bristol for what it was: a place cursed with too much time. There was too much on hand, too much to kill. Survival here demanded a habit, whether smoking or drinking or pounding down custard-filled Krispy Kreme doughnuts.

Sam and her sister, Erin, were now full-time nurses, changing diapers and sheets, while keeping track of Mom's pills, pulse, and body temp. I worked on the periphery, making runs for supplies, washing carpets and dishes. But the presence of test strips in our luggage revealed the real reason for my coming along. Late each night, far from the watchful eyes of Nurse Orlandra and Dr. Webb, Sam and I collapsed into each other's arms and used up what little strength the day had forgotten to sap. In the afterglow, we stared at a slow-moving ceiling fan and pretended to be someplace else. Bali or Venice. But Sam never let her imagination fly very far before plugging in the baby monitor that had been loaned to us by the local hospice so we could keep tabs on April at night. We fell asleep as spies, listening to a dying woman's tortured breathing — and occasional paranoid outbursts, the latter brought on by her pills. I missed our bed in Colorado, our cats and books and compact discs.

It was the presence of that monitor that caused me to eavesdrop — accidentally at first — on a private conversation. I was grabbing my wallet for a run to the grocery store when I noticed the red light glowing like a cigarette in the distance. The monitor had not been turned off from the night before, and I was reaching out to rectify this when I heard April say, "A child isn't everything, honey. Whatever problems you have will still be there."

"No," my wife replied, "a child is everything. It's all I think about some days. I swear that while things got worse for me and Tom I watched every woman for fifty miles around give birth to perfect eight-pound babies. When I learned that our neighbor was expecting her third child, I wanted to say, the bitch. And she's one of our friends."

April's breathless laugh broke up like a bad radio signal. "Always greener," she whispered.

"I wanted to give you a grandchild, Mama. I didn't want you to miss it."

I turned off the receiver right after April said, "You know I'll be there, sugar. If there's any way."

Sam's mom didn't have many more lucid conversations, because suddenly, incredibly, all that time was gone.

An ambulance came and moved April to the hospice. Sam and Erin were daughters again, no more playing nurse.

In the circle of light around April's new bed, Sam and I shared a tiny flat-bottom boat with Erin and Luther, the vast black sea on every side. The air conditioning hummed steadily; midnight had passed, and April's hungry inhalations assumed the power of ocean waves. We all stopped breathing during the last, long gap — and watched with awe, relief, and terror as her jaw went slack. I looked up at the ceiling, wanting to believe she was looking back.

The nurses came, followed by Reverend Mike and the man from the funeral home, both on call at three a.m. My father-in-law paced the room, his shaking hands in need of purpose. I led him outside. He lit a Camel.

"Damn," he muttered. "Damn."

Reunited days later with my cats and books, I was surprised by how this loss affected Sam's need for a child. I expected to hear, "We have to try harder." But five months passed before we returned to Webb's clinic.

Get your facts first, then

you can distort them

as you please.

———————————————

MARK TWAIN

CHAPTER FIVE

JINXED.

There was only one explanation. We had angered some deity and would never conceive. Like millions of other childless couples, Sam and I felt jinxed.

"Give me a break," Ellen said. "There's nothing to keep you two from becoming parents."

At the invitation of the Tu-yangs (Ellen and Jane had legally changed their last names after adopting Grace) we were spending our Saturday morning at Chinese School – a gathering of adoptive parents, their found daughters of China, and teachers that specialized in Chinese language and culture. They met every other weekend in the basement of a Presbyterian church, just outside of Niwot.

"Look, if there's any merit to your superstitious theory," she said, "why are millions of babies plopped indiscriminately into families that have no place outside of daytime talk shows? Tell me, does God have a soft spot for abusive, marginally employed self-medicaters?"

"Pregnancy has got to be the least important part of putting new life into motion," Jane said. "If we're not proof enough, then keep your eyes open. There are a lot more adopted kids living in your neighborhood than you'd ever guess."

The teachers came in bearing large cardboard posters with illustrations of animals. These were placed on a silver rail at the bottom of a wide bulletin board, which framed a map of The People's Republic. I was about to learn, if very temporarily, the Chinese words for cat, dog, snake, and lion.

We sat in a circle on the floor as the older children repeated these words, shouting proudly, sometimes gleefully, to impress their beaming parents. Little Grace smiled the whole time, and occasionally shouted, "Cat!"

Then it was Social Time. The kids played with Barbie kitchens and monster trucks and Jesus Loves Me coloring books while, spurred on by the surroundings, their parents proselytized. "I feel younger," a man easily into his fifties told me. "All the stuff I do each morning – preparing her breakfast and lunch – I know it makes no sense. I leave for work with more energy than I've ever had before."

"I treasure the sense of community," another man said. "It helps me to know we're not alone. As older parents, not just adoptive parents."

"We're here because we want Janis to understand her place in the world," a mom interjected. "We want her to be proud of who she is."

"I know she's only four," her spouse elaborated. "But we'd be thrilled if she went back to China one day to learn more about her heritage. Who knows? Maybe to help those who stayed behind."

"Well," I said, "she'll know what to say if she sees a snake."

Mom gave me a look of, *Maybe you're not ready for this.*

Although I got emotional several times that morning, Sam, for once, was unmoved. "That was interesting," she said in the car, "and the kids are great. But I want a baby, not a third language. We can't lose sight of our goals."

"Those parents sure seemed happy," I noted.

"They did seem happy," Sam agreed. "Do you think they earn commissions for bringing in recruits?"

Back in the Donor Room, I just felt tired. The models looked up at me with their soft-porn smiles, the ones that said, *I know what you're doing and I don't care. I just wish I could be there to help.*

"See you next month," the receptionist said as I departed with Sam, her slip of the tongue draining the last few microwatts of energy I'd been saving for the rest of that day. So this was how they saw our prospects.

"What's next?" I asked in the parking lot. "Automatic billing? A punch card that gives us every tenth visit free—"

Sam followed her "Got to go..." with a quick kiss. Anything to shut me up.

Work remained my refuge of choice, an obsession to offset the other one. It was better, I found, to fret about matters in my control.

Late one morning in May, however, I made the mistake of taking a break. And walking up the narrow road in nearby Eldorado Canyon State Park, I encountered three children with no more than nine years between them. They played on a jagged granite mound, showing a predilection for the rock-climbing sport that draws much older kids to the park's cliff walls. An elderly man had also stopped to observe... to the best of his abilities. He seemed cut off from the world, his eyes and ears unable to provide any sort of real sensory attachment. At least, I told myself presumptively, he's enjoying the sun's warmth and

faint hint of children's laughter, his pleasure in both augment-
ed by memory.

I kept walking, but not so quickly as to miss seeing the
smallest boy turn to face the man and shout, "Dad! Dad, look
at me!" I realized then what I was seeing: me when we finally
had our kid.

"We've been so focused on your ovaries," I said that evening over five-way chili. "It's kept me from thinking about the
parts of my body with limited warranties. My heart, my ears,
my dried-out eyes. That old guy had me asking if I'd be able
to play catch or help with homework. I doubt I'll strike terror
into our daughter's prom date. I may not be awake. Heck, I
may not be—"

"Dead would still give you an edge over half the parents out
there."

"You could be right," I said to Sam. "And really, when you
think about it, an old dead guy would scare the bad intentions
out of a prom date."

I broke off a piece of cornbread and added, "Maybe you
could prop a camera in my hand."

"I've been thinking," Sam said. "It may be time to review our
strategy."

"I've been thinking about adoption," I said.

It took her a moment to respond. "Since Chinese School?"

"Since Tennessee."

She put down her fork.

"When we were in Bristol," I said, "I studied the train wrecks
in your family in far greater detail than I ever desired. And
I had way too much time to think about the clinical depression that strikes every third LaMarr. I just don't see what's so
special about our genes. Perhaps our families could use some
fresh blood."

"Mama wasn't a train wreck. You can't say that about any of our parents."

"No, but... Since nothing seems to work." My chili and spaghetti had to be getting cold, but I knew I couldn't verify this without looking insensitive.

"There are other approaches," Sam said. "IVF, surrogacy. We've talked about these choices. Or rather, I've talked about them. You never gave any sign that you were listening."

"IV... S?"

"See. You haven't been listening. IVF is in vitro fertilization."

"You have to admit those kids at Chinese School were awfully cute."

"They were adorable. And their parents were happy. But please listen carefully as I repeat this one thing: I want an infant. I want to be there for our child's first year."

Dr. Webb was in agreement — with the wrong one of us. "It might be wise to consider the next step," he said after calling us out of the waiting room. "We could stick with A.I. a while longer, but... your chances... I wish they were better."

"You've been telling us our chances were good."

"That doesn't mean they can't be improved."

Later that day, I pulled out my copy of *Brave New World* and confirmed a long-running suspicion. Webb had not only read it, but had always dreamed of working there. "Welcome to our humble Hatchery and Conditioning Centre. Please, please, 'Doctor' is so formal. My friends call me the Director."

He caught us again the following month. "Let's hope that today's effort did the trick," he said. "But if not... I think we should be discussing in vitro." Interestingly, this was Webb's way of saying, *We are now going to discuss in vitro. Forget today's effort.*

You know as well as I do that nothing's going to come of it.

"If my practice has a specialty, this would be it."

By his own admission, Dr. Webb was a master at achieving the miraculous through IVF. There had even been a successful, if unplanned cloning in his clinic. "The cells were identical!" As for in vitro: "It's not an exact science, but our record here is impressive. I think IVF is the solution to your problem."

He talked passionately of hormonal booster shots and implanted eggs. But the odds he laid out – and tried to play down – were best described as "Welcome to Vegas." More couples went home broke and childless than broke with babies. I left his office convinced of one thing only. In vitro was not an exact science.

Come that evening, I was glad I had eaten an afternoon snack, because it was clear, standing in our kitchen, that I wouldn't be eating dinner. No sooner had Sam come home than I received the bad news: my wife had listened to a different Dr. Webb.

"In vitro seems like the logical step," she said now. "I think we should try it."

"Just what was it that didn't scare you? His math? The cost?" Sam didn't let me add, "His passion for cloning?"

"There's something you need to read," she said, holding out a pamphlet as if it were a subpoena. Webb must have slipped it to her while I was picking up the tab.

"Look inside," she said, and I obeyed. One short paragraph had been underlined. *It is recommended that most couples pursue IVF at least three times. If things don't work out to your satisfaction, you will not go through life harboring the suspicion that you didn't try hard enough.*

I interpreted these words the only way possible, that the odds for in vitro were so incredibly poor it made no sense to try just once. Yet by the next paragraph's own admission, three times hardly constituted a charm. A woman Sam's age was rewarded with a 32% chance of achieving pregnancy… and 28% of giving birth… after those three attempts.

This paragraph had not been underlined.

"At the very least," Sam said, "we'll have some closure."

"I thought we wanted a child, not $40,000 of closure." The latter, I grumbled, would cut into our savings and make it difficult to feed triplets or switch to adoption.

"You know Dr. Webb only charges $12,000 a cycle," Sam said.

I wanted to ask if she'd been sneaking out to political fundraisers. Where else would she have learned to attach the word *only* to $12,000? But, I had more important points to make. "Forget the $36,000," I said, knowing I'd *never* be able to erase that figure from my memory. "What about that inconvenient multiple-birth glitch? I don't want to be on *Good Morning America* with the LaMarr sextuplets."

"That's hardly fair. How can you say it's impossible for IVF to work, then be intimidated by a one-in-three risk of multiple births?"

"Higher for people our age," I reminded Sam.

"If our positions were reversed, you'd never let go of those numbers. All I would hear was that — statistically — multiple births never happen."

"But they do happen. The trick here is to let go of those numbers — and try seeing them as people. Because that's what they are. If a hundred couples our age go into Webb's clinic and commit to three attempts each, seventy of those couples will come back out childless and poor. As for the lucky new parents left in the pool, eighteen are never going to sleep again —"

"Twins wouldn't be bad."

"Twins would be bad, triplets worse, and anything above that suicide. The Director—"

She shot me a look of, *Stop calling him that.*

"Sorry," I resumed, "Webb will implant as many eggs as possible. He's aiming for multiple births. It boosts the odds of putting us in his portfolio of miracles. Do you know what they call the parents of triplets?"

"No."

"They call them the parents of triplets. Because the parents of triplets don't have time for anything else. Like hobbies or reading or even watching *The Simpsons*."

Bud brushed against my leg, reminding me that his dinner was late. I sensed nervousness in his motion as well. Perhaps he'd picked up on our conversation and wanted to enjoy one last meal without six identical babies competing to admit Playskool Animal Hospital's first patient.

The black and white cat made a second pass, taking me back to a time when our pets and marriage were younger. Then, Sam and I had the luxury of disagreeing on stupid, trivial things. Like when I insisted on buying a Beta VCR, convinced that VHS would soon be extinct. Or when she foolishly asserted that twelve diet sodas a day could be harmful to long-term health.

No one ever got hurt in those debates.

Bud meowed. Getting up from my chair to fetch his dinner, I regained focus. "And what would we do if five or more embryos resulted? I think we both know what Webb was talking about when he used the word reduction."

"That part bothered me," Sam said. "I'd have a hard time playing God."

"We'll be way beyond playing God at that point."

"You should read the book," she suggested. "What Jane said

about adoption applies to IVF. A lot of parents you see everyday had their babies through in vitro."

"Yeah, the ones with triple-wide strollers."

"Try to keep an open mind. Just read the book... and sleep on it."

In the interest of maintaining peace, I finished the last chapter just before midnight. This left the rest of the night for sleeping on it, a feat I could not pull off, busy as I was staring at the ceiling, popping antacid tablets, and wanting to hire a private eye to shoot photos of Webb's yacht, Porsche, and Aspen condo.

My wife and I had not read the same book.

Sam, of course, was sleeping soundly. Dreaming of triplets, no doubt, the same ones I feared running into if I somehow fell asleep.

"Those adoptive parents sure looked happy," I whispered to the back of her head.

In any moment of

decision, the best thing

you can do is the right

thing, the next best thing

is the wrong thing, and

the worst thing you can

do is nothing.

———————————————

THEODORE ROOSEVELT

CHAPTER SIX

IMPASSE.

We swap accusations, knowing full well these will escalate into threats. Three destroyers close in on Hainan, the island providing an eastern shore to the infamous Gulf of Tonkin. At Lingshui Airbase, troops surround an EP-3 spy plane, property of the US Navy, disabled in collision with a Chinese jet fighter. The pilot of that jet is reported lost, and officials interrogate the American crew, now twenty-eight prisoners of potential war. The destroyers press forward. Armageddon's in the air.

This, of course, was the lead story on Headline News when we attended Information Night at Global Chinese American Adoptions, the agency responsible for handling hundreds of successful placements each year, including one familiar to us, the one that brought Grace to Ellen and Jane.

Many of the metal folding chairs were empty. Six other couples sat with us in GCAA's reception area.

"There could be complications," conceded the agency's founder, Mr. Nu. "The politicians are playing John Wayne."

He didn't have to add, "Man, you two really are jinxed."

On the wall to our right, raven-haired girls smiled shyly

alongside new parents whose smiles showed no ambivalence. There were dozens of photos, the staging nearly identical. Most of the parents were my age or older. I didn't see the Tu-yangs.

"But all that aside, the show will go on. Everyone wants this program to continue." Mr. Nu stood before a series of poster-size prints. I recognized the artist — a child prodigy with a penchant for painting monkeys at play — from a Smithsonian exhibit we'd seen while living in Washington. Wang Yani had been twelve or thirteen at that time. Reacquainting myself with her whimsical take on the world, I couldn't help but wonder how well she'd survived both adolescence and premature fame.

I wondered, too, what we'd have to do to adopt a prodigy.

The founder was an impressive man, having built an agency respected throughout the world. It was his ultimate goal to facilitate adoptions within China, a trend he saw developing, albeit slowly, as affluent couples in Shanghai and Canton realized they had picked up yet another Western custom, that of waiting too long to start their families.

"For the time being, however, Chinese orphans urgently need willing adoptive parents in other countries." He stopped and smiled. "That is to say, you'll do for now."

Rarely during the presentation did Nu let us forget that adopting from China came with its own batch of statistics — data every bit as depressing as that dispensed by Webb. Here, the numbers were children growing up without parents — or places to live once they reached their teens. If you came to international adoption wanting to save the world, the message seemed clear, you'd better have an enormous house.

More numbers. The wait at that time was approximately two years. The girls were eight months to two years old when placement was made.

Nu walked to the photo wall and said, "These children are

beautiful and intelligent. And from everything we've observed, they're extremely well adjusted. Granted, we're several years away from seeing the first teenagers emerge in these homes, but the transition to date has been amazingly smooth. These girls do well emotionally, socially, academically." Another smile. "Many adoptive parents come back for siblings."

He talked about post-adoption depression, conceding that, yes, the blues were more common with international placements. But Nu had a solution. Love your child. Let her know she's here to stay.

He removed one of the photos from its place on the wall and held it before his face, so that only he could see it. "But again, these beautiful children are not exhibiting problems. And believe me—" He turned the photo toward us. "—you'll have no trouble finding the love they require."

———————————————

On the ride home, reviews were mixed. When I remarked that the evening had been like reading a good novel, depressing one page, uplifting the next, Sam said, "You think we should do it, don't you?"

My silence answered her question.

"I wish it could be that easy for me," she said. "Unfortunately, I walked out of that room feeling guilt more than anything." Dozens of headlights appeared in my mirror. We were pulling onto I-70 west. "But guilt shouldn't have a place in this. You can't tell me that's why Ellen and Jane adopted. They wanted Grace for the same reasons I want to hold and feed my own baby."

The semi to my left wouldn't let me in. I stepped on the gas, mumbled my dad's favorite swear wood. Gddmmt.

"I was impressed by Mr. Nu," Sam was saying. "If they really make that movie out of your novel, we should donate some of your cut."

Clever, I thought. *Just feel free to shift responsibility for saving the world completely onto my shoulders.*

"You have to admit there's more uncertainty with international adoption than there is with in vitro," she added. "I'd hate to be one of those couples right now, holding plane tickets to China. At least with in vitro, you know where you stand."

"Take me, semi," I whispered under my breath.

Six days later, Beijing and Washington settled their dispute. Sam and I did not. The hottest global hot spot was no longer on an island in the South China Sea. It was in our bedroom and kitchen, and in the front seat of our Honda Accord. More than before, I favored adoption. I wanted to be in a photo on Mr. Nu's wall. And more than before, Sam was convinced that IVF was our best last resort. She wanted to be in the *Guinness Book of Records*, her name followed by those of her octuplets. One of the boys is Tommy, Jr., named in memory of his late (dead-of-exhaustion) father.

"It's not too late to back out," said Mac as the waiter distributed our menus. My brother had invited me to lunch at M&D Ribs, and this apparently was his way of saying hello, good to see you. The dining room was baking. I was sorry I'd worn a sweater.

"Back out from what?" I asked.

"Baby World. Believe me. You don't want to live there."

I considered the source. My next youngest brother ate most of his meals alone in a Denver apartment. His one daughter lived in Kansas with "Mommy Dearest," who had raised Sallie on a religion built around hating Mac. He'd last seen her when she was twelve. Sallie was now sixteen.

"And why don't I want a baby?"

"They cry."

"Now where'd you hear that?"

"They mess up their diapers."

"That's never been proven."

"You're too old."

I had no retort.

"You need energy," my brother continued. "Parents need something to look forward to, like knowing their kids will move out someday. You'll be dead before that happens. Look at yourself, you're a dinosaur."

"Dinosaurs were powerful, intimidating critters."

"I'll be more specific. You're a Brontosaur headed for a tar pit."

It took me a minute to get out my response, "Why didn't you say this before?"

"Nobody asked."

"Nobody asked you today."

"Yeah, but I needed to say it. Because it's not too late and because you're not going to listen anyway. Because you're my brother, and so you can secretly hate me." He took a drink from his Scotch. "There's no turning back once you feel that tar oozing up around your shins."

"Come on, Mac. Do I really look that old to you? Because I sure don't feel it."

"Now, maybe not. But jump ahead 10 years. Are you gonna need a back brace to give piggyback rides? Will you end up sitting with the 'other grandparents' every time your kid gets invited to a birthday party?"

"I know older parents. They seem to be doing okay."

"Have you seen them giving piggyback rides?" Mac used a

cloth napkin to dry his lips. "I'm just trying to be honest."

"I noticed. This wouldn't be payback for all the older brother advice I've dispensed?"

He smiled for the first time since we sat down. "It's possible."

"Listen, Mac. I'm glad that what happens to me matters to you... I think. And you're not the first to express these opinions. But I'll tell you one thing right now." I paused to enjoy the nervous expression on his face. "These ribs had better be good."

He was using the napkin to wipe his brow. "So, how're the cats?"

The food was superb, and when it was gone, Mac wished me luck. "Okay. That's it. I'll never bring it up again. And who knows? Maybe you'll get a good baby. There's got to be one out there."

Back in my office, the message from Mom did little to cheer me. It was the fourth email she'd sent that morning – and the only one I opened. The others appeared to have been recycled, and Mom had taught me long before that FW means Forewarned and not, as commonly assumed, Forward. *Remember Lisa Hancock?* it began. *From Sunday School? She and her husband were having trouble conceiving. They saw a doctor. They now have two beautiful babies. Maybe you'll have the same luck.*

"When I fetch our teen from soccer practice," I said to Sam, "I'm going to be the only dad in his sixties."

"Your brother?" she said, reaching for the remote. It was movie night, and after a workday described over dinner as "grueling," Sam had been looking forward to our weekly respite.

"He thinks we're too old to be parents."

"That's a surprise."

"I know, I know. But he does have a point."

"What your brother has is a chip on his shoulder." Kate Winslet was frozen in time as Sam pressed Pause. "How old was he when he got his divorce? Was Mac too young to be a parent?"

"Even if we adopted internationally," I said, "and our child was already two when we met her—"

"You're afraid she'll be embarrassed when you pick her up after soccer? How would that make you different from every other embarrassing parent? We are not too old."

"What if we're too old to be good parents?" I said. "Other dads have energy. They have strong hearts and bones. They have... life expectancies."

"I still have energy. And I'm planning to stick around for a while. We have so much to share, so much to teach—"

"We'll have a family that skipped a generation. There are people who'd argue it's not in a child's best interest."

"We have careers we love and money in the bank. And you... you can take time off whenever you want to. We're not going to be absentee parents... or regretful parents... or bitter parents who slander each other ten years after the divorce."

I thought of Mac's daughter. "A kid could do worse, I guess."

"You don't get it," she said. "We're not going to be adequate a-kid-could-do-worse parents. We're going to be fantastic parents. The kind every child deserves."

Kate Winslet was moving again, trying to find a dry way off the Titanic. "That ship's sure taking a long time to go down," I said.

Sam stuffed a fistful of popcorn into my mouth. "Is it okay if I watch the movie?" she asked.

I managed to keep quiet for the rest of our video, but I was thinking about soccer practice. In my head I heard the squeals,

"Is that your dad?" followed by the reprimand, "I told you to wait in the car, old man. Now everybody at school will know."

I was up early Saturday, getting lost on the Internet, looking for articles and anecdotes about late-starting parents. There, to my relief, I met plenty of adults who had survived growing up alongside parents more than forty years their senior. Better yet, I found plenty of reasons to become a late starter, most of which had to do with stability. It was just as Sam maintained: older parents had solid values and relationships. They had time and patience to spare, and they had bedtimes close to those of young children.

Indeed, parents who had been forced to wait were often more caring and appreciative. There was even a risk of something called the "Special Child Syndrome," which occurred when adoptive parents cared "too much," pampering and overprotecting their children as if they were miniature rock stars. "Brandon, I am so, so sorry. Now that I know just how much the yellow Trix upset you, I will personally remove these from all future servings. And to make absolutely sure this doesn't happen again – yes, yes, you have every right in the world to keep hollering like that – I'm calling Daddy back into the kitchen and firing him on the spot." Adoption sites recommended we avoid this behavior.

As for the issue of longevity, this wasn't the concern it once was, thanks to exercise and diet. With enough broccoli and hiking, I could embarrass my kid well into his twenties and possibly thirties, critiquing career and relationship choices. I was even more surprised to learn that younger parents die, too. If anything, late starters were more likely to wear seat belts, and they understood the importance of wills and legal guardians.

Ultimately, our child would know advantages that other kids only saw in their dreams. Like when he's old enough to tell his friends, "Yeah, I know the score. My old man was giving me grief about my girlfriend, too. Some crap about loans he co-signed. But not anymore. I shipped him off to a nursing home in rural Mississippi. Saw it on *60 Minutes*; place didn't even have phones. If the old man could call, I know what he'd say. He's pretty dang sorry he ever made me eat those yellow Trix."

"You put your dad in an old folk's home?" his pals will say with a mix of envy and incredulity.

"Yeah, but it's not half the hole my uncle's in. His daughter really hated him."

———————————————

I don't know how Sam heard about it — a doctor, a friend, a notice in the paper — but we found Resolve. This was the national organization for folks dealing with infertility. The Colorado chapter hosted monthly meetings, and we were at one. As first-time guests, we paid a small fee and sat through a compelling pitch to join the club. Resolve, we were told, helped educate the infertile about their options. What's more, Resolve lobbied at the state and federal levels for insurance reform.

Best of all, in the opinion of the woman handing us an application form, it gave people like us a chance to meet others stuck in our particular corner of limbo. "You'd be surprised," she said, "at how often our members find their own solutions after being exposed to the stories of others."

I counted two dozen of these like-troubled couples, all seated at wide folding tables that took me back to the few business seminars I'd attended. The room itself, in the basement of a Denver hospital, had that same peculiar lack of ambience. The walls were empty, the color scheme neutral.

The speaker that evening was a caseworker for a Catholic adoption agency. "Be honest," the cheerful, red-haired woman advised the crowd. "Be honest with us. Be honest with your-selves. That's the only way to approach adoption — and infer-tility in general." The woman, it hit me, looked like one of our neighbors. The realtor. The one who lived just down the hill. "You can't forget how you got to this crossroads. Do you want a child? Or do you feel pressured, knowing you're supposed to have children?" Her eyes moved slowly across the audience. "Maybe you're feeling pressure to adopt. All those children in need of homes. I'll tell you one thing about saving the world. It might not cooperate. And you'll never be Mother Teresa in the eyes of your child. Just boring old Mom and Dad."

Their orphanages in Asia were flooded at that time with Vietnamese orphans. As the caseworker made clear, if you were Catholic and thought you'd make a good parent to a Vietnamese child — a worthy, all-too-real child, not some object in need of repair — you could pretty much go straight to the top of their No Wait list.

Overall in fact, if I was hearing her correctly, signing up with a Catholic agency for adoption of any kind was like cut-ting into the 15 ITEMS OR LESS lane, then having the scanner miss half of those items. The Catholics kept their lines moving, and charged considerably less than their secular counterparts. Where we'd been hearing $15,000 as the rough figure for domestic adoption (and up to forty for international), the Church of Rome advertised a four-digit fee. But there was a catch, a big one. Fake Catholics need not apply, and these case-workers didn't mess around. Not only did they conduct home audits, but they also accompanied their clients to church. The moment Monsignor took your hand and said, "Nice to meet you, I don't recall seeing you in our congregation before," the game was up.

Following the talk, we did indeed meet other couples. We

also ate cookies. With M&M's. Being there was good for me. I found comfort in seeing physical proof that we weren't alone — that many fellow travelers were also searching for that elusive child. I even felt hopeful at times, thinking that between the few hundred thousand of us nationwide, someone was bound to hit upon a solution that both Sam and I could accept.

But standing and listening, paper plate in hand, I also thought back to the years before our first miscarriage — and vaguely recalled going to parties where people discussed other topics besides ticking clocks and disobliging ovaries. No one at Resolve was asking, "Have you heard the new Keb Mo CD?" Not one man hit on my wife, or drunkenly asked me, "So you've got a book?" before revealing his plan to write a six-volume autobiography chronicling his meteoric rise to Western Regional Manager for Long John Silver's.

This, in contrast, was "I just don't understand it. All my sisters had kids by the time they were thirty."

I overheard a woman talking to Sam: "Yes, but, domestic adoption would give you an infant."

"We're open to anything at this point," my wife responded, but the pretense ended there. I never heard Sam bother to ask, "So what can you tell me about domestic adoption?"

We didn't talk much on the way home.

––––––––––––––––––––

This was where we bottomed out.

As our conflict stayed its weary course, Sam and I agreed to counseling. Five sessions in Boulder, courtesy of her workplace. To my immense relief the counselor was a happy adoptive mom with photos of her daughter all over the office. I knew I couldn't lose, and by visit number two, Birdie Kepler had thrown her support behind me. When Sam claimed that her mind was still open, Birdie smiled coyly, and I knew she could see Sam's words for what they clearly were: a desperate attempt to paint me as the close-minded one.

But the counselor surprised us both. Though I have no evidence to support my theory, I believe that, shortly before our final meeting, Birdie suffered a stroke or overdosed on hallucinogens. Outwardly, through most of the session, nothing seemed amiss. But Birdie had lost all perspective. With only seconds left to the handshake that said, Wish we could stay and chat longer, but I'm no longer getting paid for my services, the counselor calmly stated, "I think you should try in vitro."

I didn't think it was possible to panic for two weeks straight, but I was wrong. I panicked on a boat. I panicked with a goat. I panicked in the rain. I panicked on a train.

I couldn't concentrate on work or eating – and concentrated far too much when it was time to fall asleep. What do I do now? Change my name? Move to another state? I know I slumbered some, however, because I woke fairly often from nightmares about falling – specifically, triplets and quintuplets falling on me – to ask myself, Why is adoption okay for the counselor and not us? And why should in vitro work any better than artificial insemination, which initially sounded more promising? Am I the only one who paid attention in high school math?

The best thing I could say about IVF was that it had better odds than a lottery ticket. (And I wouldn't have conceded that point without adding that it was also 36,000 times more expensive.) Why couldn't Sam and her counselor friend see how it would rob us, emotionally and financially?

I recalled reading that marriage rarely survived the death of a child. Whenever one partner showed signs of swimming to the surface and breathing again, the other was waiting to grab an ankle and pull in the opposite direction. I wondered if this was happening to us. We'd lost our hypothetical child and were now holding each other down, honoring some unspoken suicide pact.

"I can't do it," I said one night in bed.

"Do what?"

"I know the vote was two to one and I'm not being fair, but I just can't do it."

"What? In vitro?"

"Of course, in vitro."

"It wasn't a vote, and even if it had been, the counselor's wouldn't have counted. I can't throw her opinion at you. That wouldn't be fair. Because the truth of it is, up to that moment I hadn't agreed with anything she said." Rolling on her side to face me, Sam smiled. "And what kind of name is Birdie anyway?"

"Adoption's the one choice that's guaranteed," I said, sending her smile back into hiding. "We've got to keep our eyes on the prize—"

"You can't take your eyes off the price. Can't you see this is more important than anything?"

I knew better than to speak, but this wasn't enough to keep me from doing so. "Than anything? How about having the money to raise our child?"

Silence from her side of the bed.

"I'm starting to miss my life," I said. "I want to go to parties and drink and act and listen to regional managers from fast food chains pitch their ideas for books."

"What are you talking about?"

"Just this," I said, knowing I should stop. "Is it worth wrecking a marriage to start a family?"

CHAPTER SEVEN
WALLS AND BRIDGES.

"You remind me of someone who used to come in here," Ellen said. "I think he was a writer. It's been ages. Rumor has it he died."

"Another urban myth," I said. "I only faked my death to build interest in the novel."

"How have you been?" she asked, smile fading. "I've been worried this baby business finally did you in. You still seeing the counselor? Is Sam still pushing for IVF?"

Taking my place on the bookstore bench, I assured her all was fine in the LaMarr household. And while this was not entirely true, conditions had improved significantly.

As such, Ellen didn't need to hear about our perfect storm of a fight. All the elements had been in place that night, making the tempest inevitable. But as the clouds rolled back, we found ourselves clinging to the same piece of debris: the realization that our marriage was the wisest commitment either of us had ever made.

"We're going back to Resolve," I told Ellen, her face partially hidden from my angle by a lopsided stack of romance paperbacks. "Sam wants to learn more about domestic adoption. And I'm rethinking in vitro." An eyebrow went up. "I may be open to trying it once, as in one time only.

"Your paralyzing fear of multiple births?"

"Invest in Maalox," I replied. "At least until we see the results. If one or no embryos implant, unload your shares that instant."

"You'll let me know?"

"It's the only time in my life I'll have insider information. And what's the point if I can't share it?"

"You've completely ruled out China?"

"Sam wants an infant more than ever."

"Tell her she can stop in Hawaii on the way."

"She's been reading about post-adoption depression. It's much less common when the child's placed at birth."

"We saw all that stuff too. And there is that worry — that an older baby won't fully bond with you. But it was more like post-adoption jitters for us."

"Some adoptive parents just grind to a halt."

"That," said Ellen, "is one way to deal with your worries. We, on the other hand, made time for Grace — we held her and read to her — which, conveniently, was all we wanted to do in the first place." She slid the pile of books to her left. "It didn't take Grace long to figure out she was our child."

Ellen put forward a theory: The older the parent, the smaller the likelihood of post-adoption depression. "When I was in high school I had this friend. Wanted a car more than anything, and her folks wouldn't help. She worked after school, saved up for two years. Finally, one Saturday morning, she pulled up to my house in a Corvair convertible."

"Corvair? I don't know much about cars and even I—"

With a scowl that said, You're missing the point as usual, Ellen asked, "How well do you think she treated that car?"

The mailman came in, bearing a bundle of catalogs and bills. "Hey, Mr. LaMott," he said. "I saw that thing about your book. Who's gonna be in the movie?"

I nearly pulled out my stock reply ("Things move slowly in Hollywood for people who aren't Stephen King. Did you know Tolstoy died without seeing any of his books turned into movies?") but realized I was tired of honesty. As such, I gave him the answer he wanted: "Last time I checked it was Marlon Brando and Britney Spears. They're each playing characters in their upper forties, so it will be interesting to see how they pull it off."

"Sounds good," the mail carrier said. "I'm looking forward to seeing what your book's about."

I thought of all those poor bastards in the Nineteenth Century. They had no choice but to read *War and Peace*.

Two days later we had dinner in Old Town with friends Carl and Penny.

"You need to check out the *Newsweek* cover story," Carl said as our appetizers arrived.

"Yeah," Penny agreed. Their three children were running from table to table, reenacting the French and Indian War. "Domestic adoption. They're saying it's impossible. All demand. No supply."

"Bobby!" Carl shouted over the asylum-on-fire howls, only seconds before his son crashed into the knees of a waitress carrying drinks. "Sorry, sorry, sorry," he said to the crimson-faced server even before the glasses finished breaking. "You'll put those on our tab, of course."

"You're sure you want children?" Penny asked.

Come Wednesday we were back in the basement of Beacon General Hospital, seated with a few dozen other couples in need of Resolve. The topic of the talk was Open Adoption. Four panelists faced us from behind a folding table: an adoptive mom and dad, the biological mother, and their go-between agency caseworker. The ten-month-old boy responsible for bringing them all together was not present, having apparently opted out of the presentation.

Sam and I had read about open adoptions, where the biological mother remains in the picture, but it wasn't the same as seeing one. The extended family on display that evening extended in three directions. By the birth mom's own count, baby was "blessed" with that many full sets of grandparents. I saw this as a cause for concern. Regular families were scary enough. No one needed an extra Grandpa or Grandma calling to insist, "You're all coming here for the holidays. It's time our precious grandson saw Wichita's Christmas Tree and Flag Parade. Gonna be something this year."

But that's exactly what this family had. As Birth Mom explained, "My folks take a proactive role in baby's development."

"I'm amazed by how well they all get along," said the caseworker, whose T-shirt framed a famous line from Wordsworth: CHILD IS FATHER OF THE MAN. Or so I extrapolated. The last three words were hidden below the table's horizon. "Absolutely amazed."

Adding to the complexity of this already complex arrangement, the adoptive parents had to be in their forties, which made Birth Mom look like their daughter — and had me asking, how would the growing child comprehend this tear in the fabric of time?

Granted, new Mom and Dad would never face a shortage of babysitters, but any notion of convenience was more than cancelled out by a surplus of interference. "Oh come on, you sissified worrywart, since when is a little beer bad for my nine-year-old grandbaby? Not like he has to drive anywhere to-night."

This was Family by Frankenstein, sewn together at all the wrong places. And even if new Mom and Dad came to their senses and chased these mutant auxiliary kinfolk out of their lives with pitchforks and torches, one core problem remained. Biological Mom. How, I wanted to know, was Adoptive Dad going to explain the young woman who kept showing up for birthdays and holidays? The one with features a lot like Ju-nior's? The one who became strangely emotional for a "friend of the family"?

Birth Mom offered her own take on this: "That can be hard. Sure. His not knowing who I am. And my having to walk away at the end of a visit, knowing he doesn't belong to me."

At times during the evening, she lost sight of this last subtle nuance. "I wasn't happy when I learned they were going to Wy-oming for his first birthday. Sure, I understand the importance for their families, but I'm family too."

"In open adoption," the caseworker interjected, "you'll find varying degrees of openness."

I for one was glad to hear this, because in my estimation the model before us was giving off a few too many of those de-grees, falling just shy of 100º Centigrade. But Dad, Mom, and Mom seemed ignorant of their proximity to that volatile point. If anything, they smiled too much and laughed too readily. One big happy big family.

When I pictured myself in Adoptive Dad's chair, however, this communal cheer was tempered, especially when one of Birth Mom's comments got to me and I finally snapped from stress, shouting, "Could everyone please shut up? I don't know what I was thinking when I agreed to this. I had more than enough family already. And Birth Mom, will you please tell *your* mom that Billy won't be raised as a Free Will Baptist."

With a shudder, I shook off these thoughts. Glancing sideways at Sam, I stole a drink from her water. It did little to ease the dryness in my throat.

A neutral party from Resolve joined the foursome, standing beside the table, off to their left. Wearing a light blue sweater that had to be warm for the room, she introduced herself as Jeri and reiterated that not all open adoptions were this open. Even so, she warned, it was always possible that a biological grandparent would start asking permission to attend Suzy's soccer games. The adoptive parents − the legal parents − were left to draw the line, and this was a pressure that few parents faced.

"Still," the adoptive mom interjected, "it's no more complicated than the divorce situations you see every day."

When Jeri asked for questions, I was quick to oblige: "Is open adoption the only thing birth mothers agree to these days?"

The caseworker stepped in to calm my nerves, saying that she handled many closed adoptions. And again, the open ones weren't all alike. Far from it. Some couples met the birth mother during pregnancy or at placement but after that simply corresponded through the agency, and only as often as both parties saw fit. They didn't share last names. They didn't share grandmas.

Jeri quickly added, "And even with a more open arrangement like this one, communication often slows and even stops after the first year or two. Things change. One party moves, or the birth mother starts her own family."

"You can be darn sure I won't lose interest," our in-the-flesh birth mother made clear.

"I won't lie," the caseworker said. "As happy as the Humphreys here are, a lot of adoptive parents pray for the day the birth mother disappears."

Mrs. H. said nothing.

Jeri anticipated the next question from me and the other six audience members with hands in the air. "Yes, yes," she said, lifting a now-familiar magazine issue above her head. "The *Newsweek* story. You need to know it's not true."

"Not true?" came a voice from behind us.

"Its authors showed a real East Coast bias. And had they worked for a regional magazine, say Southeastern Connecticut *Newsweek*, they might have been right. Because it's almost impossible to adopt in some places. Too much demand. But anyone considering domestic adoption needs to look at it on a state-by-state basis. All in all, it varies dramatically from one to the next, and we happen to be in one of the better ones. Just ask Caz here. Her agency handles about fifty placements each year, and the average wait is... what?... two years?"

"At present there are 48 couples on our wait list," the caseworker said.

"And even if you lived in one of the less hospitable states," Jeri said, "there's nothing to stop you from going elsewhere."

"I'm working with two couples from New York right now," Caz told us, leaning forward to reach her cup of water. I was right about the T-shirt; I could now read all the way to OF THE.

"It just takes research," Jeri elaborated. "Look at projected waits. How long until placement? How long before the birth parents relinquish their rights?" Sam jotted something on the legal pad she'd brought with her. I saw this as a good sign.

The remaining questions were specific to the Humphreys.

"No, of course not. We'll decide which schools she attends," Mr. H. said in response to one, before turning to Birth Mom and asking, "Right?"

The final query surprised me, not so much with its content as with its origin, coming as it did from my immediate left. Sam wanted to know, "How did you make your choice?" This, of course, was the polite translation of, "What the hell were you two thinking?"

I could have gone without knowing, because their answer scared the smugness out of me. "It wasn't that long ago," Mr. H. said, "we were sitting where you're sitting, listening to these presentations. And it wasn't all that long ago we made our choice... opting for fertility treatments. Took us through hell... and our savings."

Though he hadn't specified the nature of these treatments, I knew he was talking in vitro — the in vitro in our future. There was this as well:

"We never made it past our second try. I looked at Francine and told her I couldn't watch her go through it again. The shots and all. She was just miserable."

When I looked at the woman who had known these trials firsthand, I saw Sam in her place, and I silently recited the words of Ebenezer Scrooge. "Are these the shadows of the things that WILL be, or are they the shadows of things that MAY be, only?"

"Adoption just made sense at that point," Francine Humphrey said, pulling me back into the present. "Always had, actually. Like Dorothy in the land of Oz, the solution had been there all along."

Then it was cookie time (or as Jeri put it, "time to socialize and see what you can learn from the others here"). Sam shot off toward the front of the room where the panel had been seated. I headed in the opposite direction, toward the table with snacks and refreshments.

Holding matching green cans of soda, a young (early twenties) couple from Colorado Springs mapped out a route unfamiliar to me: pursuing adoption through Social Services. Apparently, hundreds of Colorado children were in foster care, having been justifiably removed from unstable environments. "I'd say 'homes' but that would be stretching the definition," said the woman who shared the burden with her husband of keeping the Resolve membership's median age down. "These kids need parents that give a damn."

"Now," added her partner.

The couple had been in the system less than a month, but expected fast results. By their own admission, cost had been a factor in choosing this path. El Paso County charged no fees for placement, and in fact paid adoptive parents a monthly stipend to help cover the expenses of raising a child. "We're hardly rich. Our rainy day fund wouldn't let us adopt a hamster."

There was one "drawback," he noted. Social Services represented a long shot for couples seeking infants. In compromise, these relative newlyweds — "hitched last May" — were willing to adopt a child up to four years of age.

Instead of pointing out that this wouldn't leave them much in the way of seniority, I wished them luck, and promised to call Boulder Social Services to see how it worked in my county.

Gently placing her empty soda can on the table, the woman thanked me.

"For what?"

"For not asking how we can be both young and infertile."

Her husband smiled shyly and said they had best start their long drive back to Colorado Springs.

"Boulder Social Services," she said. "Remember."

Talking — excitedly at times — two men and a woman now stood between the cookies and me. These were folks in their late thirties, more representative of the Resolve base. I moved closer, eavesdropping as I went.

The woman spoke, too quietly now for me to make out every word. But I was able to catch one thing: her comment ended with those familiar initials, "IVF."

"Everyone's entitled to an opinion," the man facing her said said in a withering tone, "...however ill-informed."

"In vitro," he continued, "is a poorly manufactured Trojan Horse. Its contents are visible through cracks and holes, but no one wants to see them." The man was too busy making his point to notice me as I took a place to his left. "Though I guess you could say a leaky Trojan's the least of our worries."

This guy looked as if he'd wandered in from a corporate sales convention with an open bar. Only partially hidden by a gray suit jacket, shirttails spilled over his belt. But this wasn't the detail that held my attention. Sometime earlier that evening, he had placed a name tag on his shirt, without bothering to fill it out, meaning it read, HELLO. MY NAME IS—

"Hi," the woman acknowledged my presence. "We're the Beemers. Fred and Sue." She took the hand of the other man, the one who had not recently attended a corporate sales convention. He nodded politely in my direction.

Then, smiling nervously, Fred revealed, "We're about to try in vitro."

"Saturday," she added.

"It's a mistake," said the opinionated man with the incomplete name tag. "Have you considered the possibility of multiple births?"

"Twins would be great," said Fred.

"I'm okay with triplets," said Sue. "We've waited so long to start a family, you know."

HELLO sneered. "Triplets? Try quints. That's what my sister had. Three pounds each at birth."

I detected sadness in Sue Beemer's eyes as she leaned forward to catch her husband's attention. She didn't speak, however. She didn't get the chance.

"You have to admit that's quite a leap—" The man's sneer was now a smile. "From fecundity to mondo-fertility."

Bravely, perhaps even altruistically, I took the heat off Sue and Fred. I announced that we, too, were thinking of giving in vitro a shot.

"Why?" asked HELLO.

"Well—" I wasn't sure I had an answer. "There's the matter of closure."

A smirk this time. I expected to hear I'd been watching too much Oprah.

"How about," I began, struggling to reclaim my dignity, "I married an intelligent person rarely prone to self-deception? If Sam feels it's worth the risks, there has to be some merit to it."

"I'm guessing it's been a long time since you needed your driver's license to buy beer," he responded. "You're thirty-eight... thirty-nine. If your wife's the same age, you're wasting your money. It just doesn't work for middle-aged women."

He had me, of course. Hell, he was using the logic I'd recently retired. And how could I argue with someone who'd shaved a few years off my age? I certainly felt no need to correct his math.

"All that aside," he continued, "what if you somehow beat the odds and IVF blessed you with four kids? I'm pushing forty myself, and I'm too damn old to feed two wailing babies at four in the morning. Age is the enemy here. Don't ever forget that. It's the enemy on every front."

"In vitro works," Fred Beemer said. "There are thousands of successful attempts. Why can't you acknowledge that?"

"Might not be so bad as a team sport." Smirk, smirk... smile. "Five couples go in together, one try only. Nine months later, the couple with quints splits up the goods. Everyone goes home a winner."

The Beemers angrily excused themselves. I heard a muttered "Jerk."

"Goodbye," said HELLO.

Just before she went out the door with Fred, Sue Beemer made sure we heard her say, "I bet no one ever asks him what his name is."

Her target didn't seem bothered. "As Robert Johnson once said—" His eyes were on me. "— don't trust everyone you meet at the crossroads."

I hadn't noticed that Sam was standing behind me – or that she'd been listening to much of the exchange. "We get it," she said, surprising me as she took the space left by Sue Beemer. "You don't like in vitro. But why dash the hopes of others?"

"Primarily," said the contentious uncle of quints, "because I'm a doctor."

"You deliver babies?"

"My colleagues do. And they're tired of watching two-pound preemies struggle through their first weeks, only to face a lifetime of residual problems."

"Do your sister's children have health problems?"

Hesitation. "Not as far as we know."

"Does she love all five of them?"

"Well, yes."

Sam stepped past the man and lifted two cookies from the tray. Handing me the larger one, she quietly asked, "Have you looked at the front of the room?"

I had. All this time, Mrs. Humphrey had been showing off photos of her ten-month-old Joey... while Birth Mom provided commentary.

I asked Sam if she had some Tylenol in her purse. She suggested we call it a night.

———————————————

Heading home, I kept my "Those adoptive parents sure looked happy" to myself. Not that they hadn't. They just hadn't done much to advance the case for *our* adoption.

Sam was the one who finally spoke. We were passing the Broomfield exit, only three more to go. "Open adoption," she said. "That sure was a lot to process. I guess every choice has complications."

"Drawbacks," I whispered.

"What?"

I reminded her that most adoptions were considerably less complicated than the labyrinthine one that had given me my headache.

"Strange as it sounds," she said, "I think the Humphreys' open adoption – their wide open adoption – was the right choice for them. But only for them."

"Right. Not for us."

"It's like we were told the first time we went to Resolve. 'Be honest with yourselves.'"

"The mantra of adoption."

"Not just adoption," Sam corrected me. "Infertility."

A metro bus shot by on the left, and I realized I was doing the unthinkable, something so out of character it chilled me to the last puny atom. With no traffic blocking me in, I was driving four miles under the posted limit.

"What are we going to do?" I asked.

Never put off till tomorrow

what you can do the day

after tomorrow.

———————————

MARK TWAIN

CHAPTER EIGHT

THE DECISION.

Four and a half years.

That's how much time had been lost. Now, with the grudging acknowledgement of one more birthday – Sam's – we were both in our forties. Officially, statistically, and emotionally, we had become an older couple, at least in that world where babies are made.

"Time's not just passing, it's passing us by," I whispered to myself, knowing I had to be stealing those words from a jingle or song.

We were in the Accord, on our way home from Snyder's Bowling Emporium. This had been the setting for "Sam's Wake," a site chosen not because Sam loved to bowl (this marked our third joint attempt) but for the practical reason that drinks were cheap. Her coworkers had organized the event, and they knew their priorities. Three twenty-five for a pitcher of Bud.

Poking at buttons in our dash, Sam cut the volume on Elvis Costello. "You know, if things had gone differently," she said, "our child would be three now." One of her gag gifts, a large-print *Reader's Digest*, rested on her lap.

"Tough birthday, huh?"

No, she assured me, it wasn't that. She had enjoyed the party, bowling included. "I never understood how important beer is to that sport."

I couldn't disagree, because Budweiser had brought out her innate pin-toppling skills... for the first 20 minutes. But that wasn't what made her smile as she recalled the evening's highlights. "We have the best friends," she whispered.

This was true as well. Several of these friends had not only crashed the wake, but had shown her just how much they wanted to be there by shelling out for babysitters.

Sam, for her part, got teased. (Boss Jeff delivered a eulogy.) She got gag cards to match the gifts. And, at the insistence of Penny and Carl and Ellen and Jane, she got bombed out of her forty-year-old mind.

But of greatest importance that night in the Emporium, Sam received several compliments to the effect of "There's no way you're a quadragenarian." And though these observations had mostly come from chain smokers growing up from barstools like stalagmites, the words rang true. My wife didn't look 40.

As I reassured her in the Accord, racing north to our suburb, she could easily have passed for 33. "In a dimly lit bar... flanked by bowling-alley fixtures on the hard side of 50... 32."

Sam didn't speak.

"I'm serious. You could easily pass for early 30s."

"Everywhere but where it counts," she said, and I figured she was referring to her ovaries, something no stranger in that hazy bar had been able to see. "Besides," she continued. "You're really old. Your opinion doesn't count."

She turned her face to the right, to the lights darting by, decking malls and family restaurants. "He'd be almost four now."

Hobbes chose the next weeks to remind us that everything changes, with or without invitation. Kitty had been throwing up more than usual. A trip to the vet confirmed he'd lost weight.

A biopsy was recommended. Fourteen hundred dollars. I wanted to say, "I'm already supporting a fertility doctor and several nurses," but didn't, of course. As you may have gathered by this point, I love my cats.

They sliced Hobbes open and told us he had IBD. I knew this was bad before the vet added, "Inflammatory Bowel Disease." If I had learned nothing else from our trials it was that initials (e.g., IVF... and let's not forget, IVF) rarely stand for anything good.

"There's one more thing. Cancer. We found cells in the lining of his stomach."

"You're—"

"Four months. Six — if he's lucky."

That night I "pilled" Hobbes for the first impossible time. Prednisone and Metoclopramide. He didn't like either. I poured him some milk, and went to bed, where I shifted uneasily and thought back to a life before responsibilities. Before job turned career. Before rent became mortgage. Back in my twenties I had been free to stay up all night, free to buy albums or books because the cover art pleased me. With friends in various stages of passing out, I watched late late movies on Cinemax, went out for tacos amidst vampires enjoying a post-*Rocky Horror* bite. I had been free all right... and lonely as only a free man can be.

Recalling those times, I felt the emptiness returning, along with a hunger for Mexican food. I got up to use the bathroom, and plodding past the mirror, saw a sad, middle-aged man staring back at me in disbelief. I thought of driving to Taco John's.

Sometime after eleven, Hobbes jumped onto the mattress, and I fell asleep scratching his belly.

Then, I was walking with a little girl. She was four or five; she was holding my hand. There was nothing extraordinary about this dream in terms of placement or plot. We were taking a detour around a fenced-in construction site.

I said, "You're my best little friend."

She said, "Why are you crying, Daddy?"

"Because—" I had difficulty getting the words out. "I used to call someone else that."

Hobbes. I was losing my best little friend.

"Sick pets, dying pets..." I heard myself sigh. We were sitting up in bed. It was Thursday evening. "We really are an older couple."

"Will you stop saying that? You've only convinced me we're a depressing couple."

I didn't share the image I'd been getting, that of a soft, poorly defined body unable to support the smooth, bald head, a line of drool connecting the lips and chin. A confused but curious being, he grows frustrated with eyes that won't focus and hands that won't grip. But his dignity suffers most from the whims of key internal organs. He can't go long without fresh diapers.

The image, of course, was of me in twenty years. "Can you imagine what it will be like when our kid graduates from college?" I said. "I can already see the other parents coming up to me and saying, 'You must be so proud of your grandchild. I said, YOU... MUST... BE... SO... '"

"Stop it," Sam said. "YOU'RE... NOT... THAT... OLD."

"I will be," I said. "Has it occurred to you we've lived our lives backwards? We're losing the quiet years, of spoiling the cats, going for long, reflective walks, and sitting on faraway beaches."

"Hobbes is leaving us," Sam said. "We can't change that."

I didn't respond.

"Our lives are changing, with or without our consent. A child will be a good thing."

This, too, had occurred to me — this being the possibility that change could be good, that my sad, predictable world might transform itself into something new and mysterious when viewed through the eyes of a child.

Sam sorted laundry while I programmed the VCR to tape Jon Stewart. On the bed's far side, socks snapped and sparked as she pulled them apart, and I waited for her to ask if I'd forgotten once again to toss a sheet of fabric softener in with the drying load.

But that's not what she said. It was rather, "There's no more time to waste."

"True," I concurred, assuming she was talking babies and not laundry. "Drastic times..."

"We need to move forward."

"Drastic measures."

And so we sprang into compromise. One round of IVF, followed by, if necessary, enrollment with an adoption agency. When morning came I signed us up for an informational meeting on domestic adoption.

I also set up a "consultation" with Dr. Webb. Though Sam would never believe me, the esteemed fertility doctor sounded giddy on the phone. "You want to talk *options*?" he said, his voice rising in pitch at the italicized word. "You know we have the means. We can make this happen."

I nearly made a third call that morning, nearly dialed a familiar number to say, "Sorry, honey, but I can't go through with this. The compromise has been compromised."

Instead, I retreated to my office and stared down my computer for more than an hour before walking to Ellen's bookstore. I had not seen my friend since Sam's bowling party. She had been on vacation, entrusting her bookstore to a substitute with inadequate training in psychiatric counseling. Today, she returned. "Great party," she said in lieu of a proper greeting. "How was Sam the next morning?"

"I keep going back to that quote you shared. Forty is the old age of youth—"

"Victor Hugo," she said. "And 50 the youth of old age."

"He'd never get hired at Hallmark."

"Nope."

We ordered take-out from the Happy Wok. Your life will adopt a new direction, my fortune read.

Ellen found this of interest.

––––––––––––––––––––

It was the middle of February, the temperature outside a pleasant sixty. The windows were cracked as we drove south on 25.

We parked in front of an unassuming office building that had probably gone up during the Savings and Loan Boom. We climbed two flights of stairs, and a young woman named Dawn welcomed us to AnAdoptionAgency. This was the domestic agency recommended most often by informally polled Resolve members (three to be exact). It also held the distinction of being listed first in the Denver Metropolitan Yellow Pages.

AnAdoptionAgency, it became clear, had earned that prized position. I soon felt at ease as, cheerfully, profession-ally, the caseworker with warm, dark eyes and long, darker hair made her case for domestic adoption. "It doesn't have to be complicated," she said from her place in front of the room, "or hard." She waited a few seconds, showing off her sense of timing to the ten-couple audience. "Provided you enjoy filling out forms and can handle a two-year wait."

The surroundings impressed me as well in that there was nothing impressive about them. The furniture was basic, the carpet worn. Fiber tape kept our table's metal legs from buckling beneath the weight of Styrofoam coffee cups, while fluorescent lights buzzed overhead and hundreds of toothless babies smiled from photos tacked to dark wood paneling as old, scuffed, and unfashionable as my original *Aqualung* album.

The AnAdoptionAgency crew was not getting rich at the expense of desperate couples, unlike, say, a certain doctor we were also scheduled to see.

Fortunately for AnAdoptionAgency, someone on their staff had realized that for every prospective dad won over by chairs that didn't match there was a prospective mom who needed more. And so we heard about experience, attitude, and commitment, most of which I found of value. But it was the methodology that surprised me most.

"We play devil's advocate when a pregnant woman contacts the agency," Caseworker Dawn revealed at one point. "If you were to witness our first consultations, you'd think we were trying to talk her out of adoption."

"Why?" I wanted to ask, though it probably would have

come out as "Huh?"

"We want to make sure they won't turn to clay when the hypothetical turns real. Let's be honest, people. Isn't this one of your biggest reservations about choosing domestic adoption? That the birth mother will change her mind at the last possible moment?"

Dawn was making sense again.

"You've got to know that for a birth mother this is as close to impossible as decisions get. It always is. We have to know her true feelings."

Dawn looked to her right, toward the wall of baby faces. "And yet, in this agency's fourteen years, only two adoptions have fallen through during or after placement."

Home in our bedroom later that night, Sam said, "I think we found a good agency."

But before I could respond, "ThatsgreatIwasthinkingtheexactsamething," she added, "I don't want to use them."

This time there was no holding back my "Huh?"

"We will if we have to. But I have to believe the in vitro will work."

———————————————————

I went on my own to Boulder Social Services, only to be mobbed by orphans. It didn't help that only three other people, three other adults, were physically present.

The kids still seemed real.

Worse, this wasn't the cast of "Oliver." These kids had been scarred — emotionally, physically, and worst of all, permanently.

"We face criticism for breaking up families," said the social worker who administered the program and facilitated the monthly orientation meetings. "Government overstepping its bounds and all that. But if you walked in our shoes for a single day, you'd want to remove ten times as many children from their homes. All these families with their vicious cycles... and more than a few vicious psychos."

The couple across from me cleared their throats in unison. They were amicable, T-shirt clad, and separated from me by yet another folding table. It was one of two in the room, optimistically placed end to end to accommodate twelve chairs. The social worker stood at the head of our table, off to my left, using up what little extra space her "conference room" had to offer. She didn't once mess with the green chalkboard behind her.

"If there's one thing this job teaches you," she said, "it's a damn tough world. Especially for children."

She'd given us forms on the way in. I looked down at mine now, trying to stay clear of the orphans' eyes. But the Foster-Adopt Program Applicants' Questionnaire had not been compiled to comfort the apprehensive. Without wasting time on politesse or triviality (Question #3. Aren't babies precious?), it insisted on knowing if I wanted children with histories of

CHECK ANY OR ALL OF THE FOLLOWING:
☐ incestuous sexual abuse
☐ abandonment
☐ fire starting

And that was only Page One.

The social worker told us the county paid foster-adopt parents a monthly stipend to cover expenses, an arrangement maintained after the adoption was finalized. It didn't matter how well off the adoptive parents were, didn't matter if they preferred NASDAQ to NASCAR.

"Cash back if you drive one home today," she said without smiling. "If you're thinking it's weird you're right. We shouldn't have to offer incentives. But as we've already established, this is one cold world."

She added, "Boulder County has twelve older children right now in need of homes."

I found it odd she'd pulled out the number twelve, because in my imagination, dozens of kids now crowded the room, twelve plus twelve plus I lost count.

"What about babies?" asked the woman across from me, and I admired the tattoo on her upper arm, a Harley-Davidson logo that matched the one on her partner's T-shirt. She wore Gwen Stefani on her own frayed tank top. She was older than the average Gwen fan. I placed her in her late thirties, which also meant she was five or six years older than her partner. The woman dyed her hair, kept it nearly as pale as her face and arms.

His reddish-brown hair was far more interesting, grown long and blown back in imitation of a rooster's crest. The face below was darkly tanned; he probably worked outdoors. As for the disparity in their ages, this he made up for in bulk. There had to be at least one X in front of the L on the tag of that black Harley shirt, though much of its girth was concentrated in the short black sleeves. This guy didn't look like he was used to losing fights. Infertility must have surprised him.

"Babies," said the woman from Social Services. "Babies are... problematic. We don't see many, and we're required by federal law to assign caseworkers to both the biological parents and the foster parents, which is what you would be the entire first year. The bio's have that time to get themselves together. If they make it through counseling, they're free to go back to abusing their offspring. File closed. It's what conservatives call a pro-family initiative. I've got stronger words for it."

"But isn't that true for the older kids too?" I said. "The part about two caseworkers?"

"In point of fact, yes. The good news for you – and more so for the children – is that these so-called parents rarely cooperate. They go into treatment for a week, then vanish."

"So what about babies?" asked the man with a mullet. "Do you have some or not?"

That's when we heard about the "two-for-one special." Apparently, only days before, the mother of a teen had tossed out her daughter – right after the daughter gave birth. As a result, two generations of this damaged family were in the county's care and up for adoption. "If anyone's interested in becoming an instant grandparent," the social worker said, "we can fix you right up."

She reached to the table for her coffee. The plastic go-cup had her name on it... sort of. MINE, it warned. DO NOT TOUCH. She took a sip, placed it back on the table. "So? That eight-year-old with a violent temper's not looking so bad, is he?"

The room had gone from warm to hot, and I felt connected to my chair, sweaty pants on plastic. I wanted to open a window. There were no windows.

I looked at the woman across from me. She seemed upset, as if insulted by the speaker's tone.

The social worker caught this too. "Newsflash, honey," she said. "When you've seen it all and then some, you've earned your right to gallows humor. It's how we survive here. Plus... my husband and I have adopted three children through this program."

The critical look disappeared.

"What about you?" The social worker was facing me; the orphans watched me, too. "I assume you're not averse to improving the world in small measures. These are children. Real children. Flesh, blood, tears, and dreams. They deserve to be wanted and safe at least as much as the rest of us." She moved closer, to the extent allowed by the table's hard rim. "The fact that you're here says a lot."

The social worker waited. "It's Tom, right?"

I wasn't sure how honest I should be. No one had ever mistaken me for Buddha or Father Damien... or even Ralph Kramden in that *Honeymooners* episode where he tries to take Alice's dog to the pound, only to rescue the others caged on death row. Though our host was correct in assuming I cared enough to attend an hour-long meeting, she was mistaking me for someone far more prone to prolonged sacrifice. I was too old, too set in my ways. My material possessions weren't fireproof.

"We want an infant," I said, hiding behind Sam. "If I come home with an adolescent my wife'll kill me."

The social worker's cell phone stirred in her purse on the floor, playing a few muffled bars of "God Bless the Child." (I had to give her credit. She really stayed on point.) What followed could have been mistaken for a fairly mundane conversation between mother and daughter, with the former telling the latter where she'd be the rest of her day. But no sooner had Mom clicked off the phone than she explained, "Mick and I can't be more than 15 minutes away from Claire. One of us always has to be in range. When she was little, Claire's biological mother abandoned her for hours on end. That was 14 years ago." The phone went back in the purse. "But you couldn't ask for a better, more loving child."

The Harley enthusiasts indicated they might be interested in adopting an older child. "We'd still prefer a baby," he added with a nervous laugh. "It'd be nice to screw up a kid on our own."

"I kinda wanted to fix up a nursery," she said. "But if that's the way it is..."

Relief hit like the first blast from an air conditioner. The eyes were no longer on me. As for my own tired pair, they had needed to witness this. It was important to know there were people like these willing to throw a little spackle on the world's rot, and in so doing, take the pressure off people like me.

They're going to be happy, I thought. *I won't see their names in the paper.* "As reported by paramedics, Mr. Harley's last words were, 'He must have disabled the smoke detectors.'"

The meeting was over. I peeled myself from my chair and picked up the questionnaire, but only with the goal of showing it to Sam.

"At least we're being honest with ourselves," I'd say that evening as she cringed at the questions I brought home from the meeting and all they implied. "I know it sounds selfish, but I kept thinking of my writing time and just how much sainthood would cut into it. Parenthood's scary enough."

"The point," she'd respond, "is that we want to know our child as an infant. We've waited too long to miss that experience."

I fell asleep that night thinking about *The Honeymooners* and how well Jackie Gleason had painted his portrait of a couple who, without ever discussing their pain, wanted children more than anything. Ralph and Alice had sure seemed happy at the end of that episode when he played savior. And yet, we never saw the dogs again.

Boulder County Social Services had reminded me how right my wife could be. It was just as she'd been saying, we needed to wrap this up and stop having our hearts broken by a damn tough world. I could only hope she was right about the other thing, the big one, that babies were good for curing depression.

I woke around three with a weight on my chest. This turned out to be a cat, but even after Bud got the attention he needed and took his leave, the heaviness remained. Bud's sweet, steady purr had not helped me forget young Claire, left alone with only the footsteps from the apartment upstairs for company, or the teenage girl evicted from her home, while holding a baby that might never know one. The sky grew light before I fell back asleep. *If the meek ever get around to inheriting this place,* I remember thinking as I drifted off, *I wouldn't exactly call them blessed.*

───────────────

Dr. Webb was promoting a specialist in Minnesota who, "for a modest fee," could specifically identify our problem. Modest, of course, meant low five figures.

"He could remove our problem?" Sam asked.

"Depends on the problem," Webb said. "He could certainly help you address it."

I waited for Sam to shout, "We'll be there tomorrow." But she didn't seem that interested in donating an extra ten grand to the cause of fertility science. "It's late in the game," she said. "What if we stuck with our plan? To try in vitro once."

"IVF. Makes sense to see," Webb said. "Of course, once is hardly sufficient. To give our methods a real chance, we need to schedule at least three attempts. You've read the literature."

This wasn't what Sam wanted to hear. "Call me superstitious," she said, "but I figure if in vitro's meant to work for us, once should be enough."

Webb persisted in pitching his three-try minimum. We didn't understand the nature of statistics, he explained, since statistically, nothing was "meant" to happen.

Sam held firm, and in the end we set a date. The first hormonal booster shots would begin late the following week, give or take a few days to accommodate Sam's internal rhythms.

"Very good," Webb said. "We're set."

Orlandra the nurse stopped us on the way out, asking if we had a minute. She offered to walk us to our car.

"Our son came to us through in vitro," she divulged as we stepped into the movie-projector brightness. "But I was 32 when I got pregnant. If you want my opinion, adoption makes sense for older couples. I see a lot of unhappy people leave this office."

Sam ground to a halt in the middle of the lot, halfway to our car, the sun hitting her face without consideration for what it revealed. Frustration, distress. A stone-solid tiredness. All of which she took out on her keys, now being squeezed with the force used by the TV-series Superman that one time he made a diamond from coal.

"You don't think we should go through with it?" said Sam.

"I don't think it will work," the nurse replied, matching the sun for honesty. "I only know what I've seen here."

Sam blinked her eyes, but did nothing to shield them.

"It hurts for me to say these things," Orlandra said. "But not half as much as it would to sit by and watch."

Though my wife failed to mention it, we were close to scuttling our compromise plan. Maybe she hadn't known either. But it took only one more person to talk her out of in vitro.

That was Fred Beemer.

Two months had passed since we first met Fred and Sue at the tail end of a Resolve meeting. Now, to my surprise, they were hosting the "living room support group" we'd traveled into Boulder to attend.

Unfortunately, I didn't have to ask them, "Weren't you about to try in vitro? How'd it go?" The answer was manifest in their presence as hosts.

Fred told us that he and Sue had been married three years. This was his second — and final — union. "I never wanted children with my ex. Now, with Sue, it seems only natural." Fred was an eco-chemist, Sue a holistic veterinarian.

"We're going to try surrogacy," he volunteered next. His specimen would be used to impregnate a stranger's egg. A woman in Denver had already agreed to carry the child.

"Sounds complicated," I said, veering away from my first word choice, desperate.

I understood desperate, of course, and I understood the mechanics of surrogacy. But I had never met anyone even vaguely considering the method as a real-life option. I knew there were two variations, scary and ultra-scary, and that Fred had described the horror show extreme. The other involved collecting both sperm and egg from a prospective set of parents, while still farming out the time-intensive manufac-turing work. In this milder PG-13 version, the pre-fertilized egg is implanted inside a womb belonging to a woman very much like the one the Beemers had under contract. She is young, she is healthy, and she views pregnancy as a less demanding way to work off a college loan than waiting tables.

"We saw a specialist after the IVF failed," Fred said. "He ascertained that our problem was with Sue's eggs."

"Have you looked at adoption?" Sam asked.

Fred answered too quickly: "I don't think I could love a child not genetically my own."

I knew Sam was thinking the same thing I was. What about Sue? She's not getting a child that's genetically her own.

Perhaps knowing that he'd made himself look insensitive, Fred related the story of an adopted nephew who had never fit into the family. "Constantly in trouble. A bad apple."

Needless to say, these words did little to restore Fred's sensitivity rating.

"And what if you get a bad egg?" I asked.

"Surrogacy won't be easy," he conceded. "IVF was traumatic enough. And we don't have the resources for repeated attempts."

Sue called from the kitchen, "Honey, I need a hand out here," and Fred excused himself.

"I should've listened to you and brought the wine," I said as Sam reached down to place a slice of quiche on her paper plate. "I could use a glass after that."

We stayed for nearly two hours, conferring, snacking, and of course when required, supporting. We met a couple new to the trek, still on their first fertility specialist. "Did Clomid ever give you really bad hot flashes?" the woman asked Sam. We talked with an insurance agent named Paige who was about to adopt from Ecuador. "The single mom bit's pretty daunting," she said. "You bet. But it's going to be a family affair. My sister lives nearby, and Mom's in Broomfield. I'm counting on them to make this a little less impossible."

Yet, I couldn't stop thinking about the Beemers' impending experiment in surrogacy. If both Fred and Sue felt comfortable with the choice, where did I get the right to be critical? They, after all, were the only ones familiar with the dark, constricted pathways that had brought them to this place, which they chose to see as a clearing in the forest. Inwardly and outwardly, I wished them well, just as I had when they were waiting to try in vitro.

Sam had reached a different conclusion.

No sooner were we in the car than I heard her say, "What's so special about Fred Beemer's genes?"

"What's so special about anyone's genes?" I said, reviving an unpopular opinion. "When was the last time Hank Williams, Jr. — with the emphasis on Junior — wrote a song like 'I'm So Lonesome I Could Cry'? And what about history's greatest irony? Have you heard the one about the lowly playwright who obsessed over the absence of a male heir? He was afraid the Shakespeare name would perish."

Sam floored me with her next words, mostly because they belonged in my speech. "If the Beemers had any sense, they'd see that adoption is the obvious choice. They're already halfway there."

"True enough," I said, about to play devil's advocate and wondering why. "But there's no way I'd wish Fred Beemer on an adoptive child. His bad-apple remark had 'self-fulfilling prophecy' written all over it."

Sam didn't say another word until we stopped for a traffic light. "You still think we should go straight to adoption?"

"You're having second thoughts about in vitro?"

"More like eight-hundred-and-twenty-second thoughts."

Was I really hearing this? Had Fred Beemer succeeded, albeit inadvertently, where I had given up?

"What if," said Sam, "instead of in vitro we tried artificial insemination one last time? It would seem like a bargain at $750, but that's not our reason for doing it. I'm thinking more in terms of divine intervention. This would be our way of saying, 'Dear God, if we're supposed to have a biological child, now's the time to speak up.'"

She said one more thing: "You can go now."

"Hmm?"

"The light turned green some time ago."

I let the van behind us honk. And reaching over to take Sam's hand, I asked if she was sure.

"As sure as I've been about any of this."

I knew I should feel sorry for her, letting go of the dream she'd clung to for so long, the dream that came true so easily for others. But Sam looked happy, excited even. We were moving forward. We were going to be parents, one way or – lacking divine intervention – the other. I held her hand more firmly than before as we swam to the surface and breathed in for the first time in months.

Well begun is half done.

ARISTOTLE

CHAPTER NINE

AUDITIONING FOR PARENTHOOD.

"Looking good," said Orlandra as she hunted for eggs on the ultrasound screen. "I'm excited for you."

"You are?" Sam asked with more than a hint of incredulity.

"I just know that however it happens, you're going to end up with the world's coolest kid."

She identified two eggs.

"Excellent. Excellent."

But not meant to happen through artificial insemination. We didn't get pregnant.

For me, the only surprise was in Sam's reaction. She didn't seem that bothered.

The Friday after we knew the outcome, we barbecued shrimp instead of ordering our weekly three-topping pizza. We also emptied two bottles of wine, crawled upstairs, and took back our sex lives.

"Purple Rain" never sounded better, and as the last notes dried up and our CD player whirred to a halt, Prince was replaced by a Chopin nocturne of a breeze coming off the mountains and through our balcony door. "The next specialist we see," whispered Sam, "will be a pediatrician."

After waiting so long, she now had her closure. Our application had been mailed to AnAdoptionAgency, as had a check that would have made Webb happy. Nearly $8,000, the first of two payments, with the second due at the end of the process. The sum was non-refundable, our contribution to the cause of adoption. If during our wait we became pregnant, divorced, or unemployed, that was our problem. See ya later, kind donator. The money would stay to help others in the pool.

That said, it was one of the easier non-refundable checks for just under $8,000 I ever wrote. AnAdoptionAgency practiced fairness, and this put us at ease. If a birth mother required medical care in her third trimester, the agency provided that help. If housing was an issue, likewise. Disbursements came out of the pool; the adoptive parents were not presented with an invoice, Oops... one small complication. Balance due $52,000. The agency worked with averages. They knew what expenses were involved, and how to spread these evenly.

We were pursuing a semi-open adoption. We would meet the biological mother two or three times, beginning most likely before she gave birth. We would not share last names. Then, after placement, Sam and I would provide the agency with six-month updates, in writing and photography, on baby's progress. Our caseworker would forward these to the birth mother.

"One more thing to remember," Dawn stressed in our first private session. "You're not buying a baby. The birth mother's not selling a baby. We pay expenses, nothing more. If she asks for money beyond that, we have to explain there's just no way."

I started to speak but Dawn had me figured: "You also should know this is the one thing we're not allowed to joke about. Ever."

You might have thought they'd be happy with the check. But AnAdoptionAgency wanted more, pages and pages more. They wanted tax returns and bank statements and medical histories and police records and notarized affidavits proving we returned our video rentals on time.

They also wanted autobiographies. And so, sitting at home on a sure-looks-nice-out Sunday, we answered dozens of prying questions about our marriage, childhoods, and emotional scars. *Number 18: No, how do you really feel about your mom?*

Defending our lives might have been easier had the queries been multiple-choice. AnAdoptionAgency favored detail, the kind that resulted in truthful slip-ups. There were vast blank squares beneath each question, leaving plenty of space to confess if we'd cheated on taxes, or diets, or each other.

Had I ever forgotten to water the plants? Had I smoked pot, and if yes, had I inhaled?

Had I ever killed a man just to watch him die?

"This is worse than the stuff I get asked before giving blood," I said over lunch, the forms still concealing the kitchen table's surface. "It's as if we're no better than Supreme Court nominees in front of a Senate committee."

Sam's eyes had glazed over, ice on blue water. She hardly touched her sandwich.

"You have to admit one thing," I said. "They're good at making you think. I realized this morning I've never really forgiven brother Eddie for doing wheelies on my head with his twenty-inch Stingray. Doesn't matter it happened decades ago... when I was ten... in a nightmare."

"This doesn't piss you off?" Sam asked. "What business is it of theirs how Mama and Daddy got along when I was a kid? Or if they used spankings for discipline?"

"There's no denying these questions eat fur balls," I said. "But

I'm trying to look at it from baby's point of view."

"Really? And what does baby have to say?"

"That all prospective parents should be duly grilled. Might weed out the monsters."

She congratulated me on my ability to rationalize virtually anything away. "Of course," she added, "that's just my point of view."

Three hours later, I came to doubt my logic. That's when I saw the final question, the one that wasn't really a question. *Describe your spouse's strengths and weaknesses.*

It was time to plead the Fifth, just as I had for numbers 4, 8, 9, 26, and of course, 32.

Describe your spouse's weaknesses. Yes, Ma'am, without delay. Better to admit that, as President of the United States, I invaded Iraq for the sole reason it was the only Middle Eastern country with a name I recognized.

"We have something for you," Ellen said as I walked into her store.

"You found a signed first edition of *Huckleberry Finn* for under twenty bucks? I knew you'd come through."

"What kind of gift would that be for an infant?" she said. "I know we're jumping the gun, but Grace saw it and insisted."

"It's Barney," came a voice from behind the counter. "From TV."

"Thank you, Grace," I said as she emerged. "This will be the first thing to go in our nursery."

She held onto the purple dinosaur, needing to play with him a bit longer before setting him free.

"Well?" Ellen said. "You're happy with your choice?"

"The cats[2] are getting suspicious."

"I was thinking more of you and Sam."

"It's taken ten years off our marriage," I said. "But I have to admit, the paperwork nearly did us in."

Ellen smiled. "For us, it was our police record."

"You have a police record?"

"A neighbor of ours filed a complaint about barking dogs." She waited a second before adding, "Four years before we began the adoption process."

The People's government, she elaborated, didn't share their fondness for pets, especially when coupled with "deviant sexual orientation."

"That last part's the funny one," she added. "They can't see a solution to overpopulation when it's staring them in the face."

"In some ways," I said, "you had it easy."

"You're kidding, right?"

"We had to play God."

Her expression let me know she wasn't impressed.

"I'm serious," I continued. "You wouldn't believe the questions they gave us. What would we or wouldn't we accept? How much could we tolerate in the way of behavior and genetics?

"Thou shalt not permit schizophrenia in a birth parent's history. Dittoeth for Down syndrome. But what about rape? Binge drinking? Crack? The list went on and on – and never lightened up. Paraplegia. Incest. HIV."

"Wow," she said. "Playing God."

"Without the benefit of omniscience," I noted. "We were pretty open. But it sure got tiring, saying no, no, no to everything we couldn't handle."

2 The plural cats indicates that the LaMarrs are capable of bearing good news. Up a few ounces and much more active, Hobbes was baffling the experts. But I knew what had changed. He now had a goal in his life – to outlive his vet.

Ellen gave me a hug, and Grace followed suit. I felt Barney pressed against my knee. "But you are saying yes. You're agreeing to love and raise a child, a child as worthy of love as any other."

"You're not disappointed with us for choosing domestic adoption?"

"Is that what you've been thinking?" she said. "Sure, we've been pushing international, but that's only because our own experience was so rewarding. Adoption's always a good thing."

Penny got emotional when she heard the news. "That's great. Domestic adoption. I'm so glad that magazine was wrong. You two are going to make the best parents."

Back from visiting family in Nebraska, she and Carl had stopped by after dinner. The kids were at home watching Harry Potter with their Aunt Thelma, who had stowed away in their van for the return trip.

"You're one of our references," Sam told Penny.

"Don't be afraid to use words like saint and hero," I said. "I'm willing to make it worth your while."

"You know we'd lie for you," Carl responded. "But we have our limits. Nice guy might be doable."

"You wouldn't believe the forms," Sam said.

"Or the classes," I added. "Or the home visits."

"Our first one's next Friday," Sam told them.

"Time to thin out the liquor cabinet," Carl said. "If you need help, I'm here for you."

"The home visit should be easy," I said. "Our caseworker's great. Down to Earth. Good sense of humor."

"What's giving us the jitters is that we're supposed to write letters," Sam said. "As in, write. By hand. And we have to create a video about our lives — all to be seen by prospective birth mothers."

"So you're auditioning?" Carl said.

"You've got it," I said. "We're auditioning for parenthood."

———————————————————

Dawn didn't even notice how well-stocked our liquor cabinet was. Or perhaps she didn't care. The caseworker seemed perfectly satisfied with filing a report that noted the absence of underfed Rottweilers and open-pit mines in our backyard.

The toughest question she asked during the visit was, "Where are you going to put the nursery?"

We were sitting in the front room, plying her with cookies from a bakery on Main Street. Peanut butter. Chocolate chip. Imitation Oreos the size of pizzas. She wrote something in her notebook, which had to have been, *Adoptee could develop weight problem.*

"Any tips on writing the letters or making the video?" I asked.

Dawn reached into her briefcase to retrieve several photocopied letters and three videos, the latter in plain white cases. "These samples are from couples who are no longer childless." But this didn't mean the letters or tapes should be seen as blueprints. "We're talking tricky business. Especially with the videos. You should trust your own instincts."

She promptly contradicted this advice by handing us a sheet of requirements.

Sam read aloud, "Videos must be eight to ten minutes in length. Anything longer than ten minutes will be returned for editing to meet the time guidelines..."

Both Dawn and Sam gave me funny looks when I whispered to myself. This kept me from revealing I now had a working title for the project. *Our Lives in Ten Minutes or Less.*

Sam resumed, "Videos must be submitted with a duplicate copy. Families are encouraged to have scenery changes in the video. Feel free to show your family involved in activities, hobbies, with your pets, in your home, etc. Videos must be completed and available for viewing within 45 days of the family study being approved. Please incorporate the following topic areas:

- ☐ How extended family feels about adoption
- ☐ Career field
- ☐ Interests and hobbies
- ☐ Dreams for child
- ☐ Helping a child understand adoption

I looked to my left to see Bud spying from the kitchen. His eyes were yellow and hard, coldly condemning, and I felt like a mouse who had strayed too far from his hole. How much had the Bud Cat heard?

Dawn told us she was constantly surprised by some of the reasons birth mothers gave for their choices after watching these videos. Her favorite example? One very young woman liked the couch she saw. It reminded her of the couch at Mom's.

"We have couches," I said.

"Then my advice to you is flaunt those couches," she said. "Pets are good, too. We hear that all the time from the women these are made for."

Dawn told us that the grounds for rejection could be interesting, as well. Some birth mothers heard the pleas of older couples and concluded that spoiled baby boomers were capable only of following their own selfish schedules and couldn't have wanted a child that badly.

"At the same time, if you emphasize how hard you've tried,

your age becomes an issue. A pregnant nineteen-year-old might watch and say, 'They're older than my parents,' or, 'They won't be fun parents.'"

We found these words troubling, and would replay them in our heads for hours after she left. On the other hand, we now had a theme for our video:

"We will be fun parents, dammit."

Remember when

life's path is steep

to keep your mind even.

_____

HORACE

CHAPTER TEN

BURNING UP IN REENTRY.

Eighteen to 24 months. This was the projected wait. Sam and I were 39 on the list.

"We're going crazy," a woman with a number much lower than ours confided during our first education class. "Every day for two years I've walked past the nursery. And every day for two years it's been empty."

I could have asked what this had to do with our group exercise. Sitting in a circle of six, we were supposed to be discussing ways to discipline young children. But what she was saying made the topic seem irrelevant.

"We're five on their list," her husband joined in. "Same as we've been for the last few eternities."

This couple, I could see, was burning up in reentry. Launched into space on the wings of bold promise, they'd been up there too long, and the thrill of new momentum had since given way to emptiness and doubt.

I looked over at Sam and knew she was thinking the same thing I was. We wouldn't set up a nursery till there was a baby to go in it.

I had one more thought: We wouldn't ask Couple #5 to join us for lunch.

"We've been trying to maintain a sense of optimism," I said.

"It's not something that comes without effort," Sam added. "For either of us."

"We keep telling ourselves the adoption will happen when it's supposed to happen," I said. "We're trying to enjoy the things we're giving up, like sleeping past six on a Sunday morning."

"That worked for us the first eight weeks," the woman said.

"Yeah," said the spouse. "Optimism gets old."

And when we come back from lunch, Sam and I will disguise our faces and sit with a different group.

"We're going to die childless," the woman said next. "Put it on our tombstones. Number Five on the list."

Her husband played with a crumpled napkin. "The hell of it is, our nursery's no longer the problem. Every room's a waiting room."

Education Class was mandated by the State of Colorado. Sixteen hours total. Twenty-four for international adoption.

And so we were back at AnAdoptionAgency on a Saturday morning. In the light of east-facing windows, the tables with taped-up legs looked even mangier — hammered and gouged and magic-markered, the kind of furniture Salvation Army crews refuse to pick up at curbside. Once again, the décor gave me comfort.

We shared these tables with sixteen-and-a-half other couples. (A teacher who planned on becoming a single mom accounted for the fraction.) Dawn shouldered most of the teaching chores, but these were lightened throughout the day by other caseworkers and "outside speakers."

A legal expert filled us in on the details of Colorado state law as it applied to adoption. Under that law, Sam and I would be foster parents the first six or seven months we knew our child, and this entailed risk. "Low risk, true," Ms. Waxman quickly added, "but nevertheless, quite possibly the greatest emotional risk you'll ever know."

Soon after we took our child home, she explained, a notice would be posted in an effort to locate the birth father (unless, of course, he had already relinquished his rights as a parent). If he materialized within three weeks, he won the right to challenge the adoption in a county court. We probably wouldn't like that.

"But don't forget what I'm about to tell you," the expert said. "This almost never happens. And when it does, we present the stronger case."

Five months after placement, Sam and I would be due in court to show we were ready to drop the *foster* preceding *parents*. AnAdoptionAgency staff would do most of the talking, and the judge would already be familiar with our backgrounds.

"I repeat," said the expert, "the risk is low. But nothing's over till it's over, and you could wait as long as two months to receive the revised birth certificate."

"Let me get this straight," a woman sitting behind us said. "The wait we just started is followed by another wait?"

"Correct. But I'll say it again. This agency has an excellent record of success. From the moment your baby goes home with you, I suggest you think of him exactly that way. As your baby. Parenting is never risk averse. If you want something safer you should take up bank robbing or shooting heroin. Believe me, I know. I've raised two girls."

She finished by telling us something I already knew from

using the Yellow Pages: AnAdoptionAgency maintained a small office in Jefferson County. What I had not known was why, and this proved far more interesting. As Ms. Waxman explained, "We know the Jeffco courts and they're very sympathetic toward anyone wanting to adopt.

"Furthermore," she said, "there's a county-wide newspaper that's ideal for posting our notices to absentee birth parents." She didn't have to add, "Nobody reads the damn thing."

That afternoon, our class was introduced to Margaret, the agency's founder. Margaret was older, officious. I liked the fact that she was in her fifties. Everyone we'd worked with up to that point had been younger than us by at least a decade.

Speaking with a British accent dulled by time, the woman with auburn-red hair and Ben Franklin bifocals gave us tips on talking with children about adoption. Basically, there were two: "It's never too early to start using the word around your baby," and, "Apart from that, you have to be very precise in what you say."

She told us about the adoptive parents who comforted their son with the words, "Your birth mother chose adoption because she loved you." The boy shared that revelation with his friends, and they in turn were terrified. They lost interest in play and *Sesame Street*, they didn't want dessert, and when they woke from nightmares they made sure everyone else on their streets woke up as well. All of which remained a mystery until one of the boys asked his mom about a tale he'd been told. A horrid account, far more frightening than *Hansel and Gretel*. After all, even the Brothers Grimm had known better than to end a story with the moral, When mommies love you they give you away.

Margaret shared other examples of adoptive parenting gone bad, all because of poorly chosen language. "It's a matter of forethought," she said as she distributed stacks of reading material. "There are more wrong ways than right ways to talk about adoption.

"Not to worry," she added. "We're all going to be good mums and dads."

Our day ended with the fundamentals of caring for a baby, which seemed a lot harder than it should have. But my brain had become an overloaded dump truck spilling gravel on the cars and blacktop behind it. When a guy volunteered to get up in front of the class and change a diaper on a true-to-scale baby doll, I could only wonder, *"How am I going to remember all that?"*

———————————————————

In preparing to make our video and prove beyond doubt that we'd be fun parents (dammit), Sam sorted through our photos, pulling out only enough to cover every flat surface in our house. This was because the sample videos on loan from Dawn employed still images to break up the dialogue — and illustrate themes like family togetherness and "Gee, look what nice things we own."

As such, Sam collected photos from whitewater rafting trips and our one failed attempt at downhill skiing. There were shots of us standing on mountains, of me jamming with Erin's boy Jake on acoustic guitars, of Hobbes balancing precariously on a telescope stand. Everywhere I turned, I saw fun people doing fun things, always in the company of nephews, nieces, siblings, and cats, an extended family orbiting like electrons.

We had a director for our film. This was the good news. Without any prompting, Carl had volunteered services we didn't know were his to volunteer. I hired him on the spot after seeing his first credential. He and Penny owned a camera.

Luckily for us, his resume didn't stop there. Carl loved making videos as much as he loved watching movies, and a friend of his happened to be a professional "video artist" who owed him a favor. "I'm sure I can get him to edit ours for free." Carl was offering to save us at least $1,200 – the starting fee for hiring one of the specialized video production companies that advertised to adoption agency clients.

Penny provided the reference. "Carl loves his camcorder."

At our first pre-production meeting, otherwise known as brunch at our house, Carl simplified the process by suggesting we write an outline instead of a script. "Those sample videos you loaned me," he said. "I couldn't believe how stiff everyone was. Heartfelt. That's what we're after. Not recited. We want this to flow. And blend seamlessly. Like... have you ever seen those Ken Burns documentaries on PBS?"

"You don't think that's aiming high?" I asked.

Carl didn't answer, and it was clear he didn't think he was aiming too high. He wanted to produce something worthy of pledge week.

"Then I hope you're getting actors to play us."

"No worries," he said. "We'll pull it together in the editing stage. How's Saturday look for the shoot?"

On Friday, brother Mac drove up from Denver to collect Sam's photos, which he'd promised to digitalize using his scanner. We paid him up front with pizza from Cortino's.

Over mushrooms and Italian sausage, I told Mac that my freelance work for advertising clients was finally going to prove good for something. "A marketing strategy," I said. "We're not going to look desperate. We're going to show birth mothers that we love our lives, and that a child would only add to the bliss."

"Always stress the positive," he said. "First rule, right? You don't sell tuna with desperation."

Two drinks and several subjects later, I said, "Mom's already sending emails asking if there's good news. I'm not sure we can handle that for two full years."

"It could be worse," he informed me. "She sends me megabytes of stuff about my girlfriend from high school. 'Divorced again.' That's how the last one started. 'Maybe you should give her a call.'" He paused to sip his scotch. "Do you think she's hoping I'll move back into my old room, put up some Led Zeppelin posters, and re-enroll at Senior High?"

I got up to change CDs. "Listen to us. Is this how my kid's going to talk about me one day?"

"Only if you teach him to speak," Mac said.

All during Saturday's video shoot, Bud and Hobbes hid in the basement like Hollywood prima donnas refusing to come out of their trailers. I should have followed suit. Each time Carl said, "Roll," Sam and I turned into the heavy kid with braces called before Bloody Mary O'Connor's fifth-period history class to give a speech from note cards smeared by sweat. Though glad we didn't have strangers coordinating the video, I couldn't have been more self-conscious blabbering about the love I was ready to give our child, all the while looking at Carl.

Making it worse, whenever we taped outside, our awkwardness wasn't the only thing that started on cue. Each time Sam or I began to say something remotely worth saving, dogs barked from three directions and airplanes attempted to land on our roof, as if yanked out of the sky by some magnetic pull in the camera's microphone.

And each time Carl finished a shot, he said, "Great, just great." But I could tell he wanted to cry.

The following morning, Sam and I watched our screen debuts.

"We look like robots," she said from her side of the bed.

"Nervous robots," I added. A hummingbird hovered near the sliding screen door to our balcony, sun glinting on its wings to form mostly transparent triangles. He stayed just long enough to remind me that everyone else in Colorado was out hiking alongside silver mountain streams on this Sunday morning taken straight from a commercial for Coors.

"Hopeless," I said as the last scene sputtered to an end. "I think we have about one good minute. That leaves a few holes in our outline."

"Not ready for prime time," Sam muttered.

"Not ready for local access cable. Watching this stuff is more depressing than shooting it was."

The one time I spoke with any eloquence whatsoever, Carl had gone for a wide shot. As a result, when quasi-articulate Tom appeared, he was seated on a couch while a huge black shoe bobbed up and down in time with his words.

In another scene, wild dogs attacked Sam from just off camera. It was all the microphone had picked up. Luckily, a squadron of B-52s swooped in to destroy them.

"No one's going to choose us," Sam said quietly. "We're going to be that couple we met at class."

We stared at the screen, which was now gray static.

A familiar high-pitched ring finally broke our trance. The hummingbird had returned.

"Let's go for a walk," I said.

We were circling Harper Lake, two blocks north of our house, savoring what little we could of that otherwise savorless weekend. This was a lake so quiet and blue, and so out of place at the top of our mesa, it could only be called a man-made reservoir. "My personal Lourdes," I said as we passed the approximate halfway mark, a black iron bench that faced both water and mountains. "When a paragraph takes ill and doesn't look like it's going to pull through, this is where I bring it."

I stopped to assess the Continental Divide, still stubbornly hoarding last winter's snowfall. In tens of millions of years, these mountains had seen it all, creation, extinction, slaughter, growth. None of which meant jack to the peaks, such is the indifference of stone. They certainly took no interest in matters as small as my existence, though at one point, I could have sworn I heard Long's Peak whisper, "Bet you wish you were up here hiking like everyone else in Colorado."

"Voiceovers," I said.

"Say what?"

"It's not too late to script some dialogue. We could dub it in the studio, then use it over some of the photos. And what about that footage Carl shot in the park?"

"Hmm," she said, tacitly agreeing we were better at sliding down slides and swinging on swings than at extemporizing before cameras. "What would we say?"

A family of geese, six in number, swam from shore, dividing the water into mirrored patterns of widening ripples, like butterfly wings that went on forever.

"I don't know," I replied. "But we *will* have a script."

The geese were half a lake away, black specks against overwhelming brightness, an archipelago of sunspots. "A script," Sam said. "I'd like that."

Carl's dream of winning the Emmy for Best Documentary

Influenced by Ken Burns slipped further and further away.

Early on a Saturday, the three of us drove for more than an hour, racing south to Castle Rock to meet Carl's video artist friend, Stu. But once we were in Stu's basement studio, he didn't seem to fully appreciate our sacrifice. Five weeks into being a brand-new dad, he had not been sleeping, well or at all, and he didn't have the patience for subtlety. "What exactly did I agree to?" he asked Carl.

His question, unfortunately, became more relevant as the morning slogged on and we gradually learned that none of the material in my tote bag was compatible with Stu's equipment. He didn't have jacks for the player that carried the theme music I'd created, nor did he have inputs for Carl's camcorder.

"I suppose we could download the photos," Stu said. "If only to save this morning from being a total waste." But the CD my brother had made refused to yield its contents.

"What if we redid the music?" I offered. "I brought my Les Paul."

Stu spoke tersely: The footage needed to be transferred one way, the music another, and the photos needed to be scanned on "professional" equipment. The kind we'd find at the local Walgreens.

One last thing. We needed to get the hell out of there and leave Stu alone. And while he hadn't actually uttered these words, we knew that's what he was thinking.

But he surprised me by saying, "Let's see the guitar."

Stu was a musician — bass and drums — I knew this from Carl. And now, with his third cup of coffee kicking in, Stu suggested we "might 'swell adjourn to the music room and play a few songs."

"You gotta know 'Rocky Mountain Way,'" he said, and the slide bar that had been in my guitar case for decades came out for an overdue encore. Sam and Carl picked up maracas.

"Great bass," I complimented Stu.

He seemed to be thawing.

"Wow, what's that?" he asked as I started another song. "'Down by the River'?" Two verses later, my frustration took musical form and I did the impossible, adding a new layer of sloppiness to Neil Young's primitive, angry solos.

Stu did something impossible himself.

He smiled.

"Why don't you take a few weeks and make sure everything's ready?" he said as the final E-minor chord oozed from his amp like dirty motor oil. "I think we can make this work."

———————————————

The Friday before we returned to Stu's studio (which only sounds like the title of an ancient Phil Collins hit), Stu called to make sure everything was ready.

Was the raw footage available?

Were the still photos scanned?

The music?

"To be honest, I'd always wanted a camcorder," I said. "This gave me an excuse to buy one. For the sake of my child, of course."

Three weeks had passed since the first fiasco. Driving back to Castle Rock, we learned that in offering us another chance, Stu had been motivated by something larger than a shared familiarity with an obscure Neil Young track.

Stu, Carl said, was adopted.

"Seriously?" said Sam.

I wasn't that surprised. The information fit in with something we'd been learning about the world. Much of it was adopted. The more we told others about our decision to pursue domestic adoption, the more others told us that they had adopted — or had been adopted.

Stu seemed happy to see us.

He also seemed to have downed several cups of coffee.

"I've got some fresh ideas," he announced as he hurried past his wife, who with baby in arms was trying to say hi. Sam offered her a bagel from the box we had picked up en route. "Thanks for letting us borrow Daddy," I heard Sam say.

Seconds later, we were in the basement, standing before microphones on long silver booms and reading the voiceover parts we'd written.

"Good," said Carl when we were done, a hint of surprise in his voice. Stu nodded and reached for his coffee.

When Sam squeezed my hand, I knew she was saying, "Thank heavens our acting career is over."

After downloading the music and photos, Stu showed us our outline, now a computerized flowchart with color-coded bars representing the spoken segments, photographs, voiceovers, and music.

He then began turning knobs and punching keys, slowly transforming our raw materials into something considerably less embarrassing. As if holding an invisible brush, Stu painted over the seams and splotches.

Sam and I watched mesmerized.

Stu was a digital artist.

He played with the sound on segments that, to my ears, seemed unsalvageable. As if by magic, the jet planes flew out of range, leaving Sam's speech to fill the void.

Whenever the story's arc sagged, Stu pulled up the music for background support, just like in the movies. Attention, audience, you're supposed to cry here. He added a title over the photo we'd chosen to start the presentation, and I couldn't find reason to complain as *Our Lives in Ten Minutes or Less* became the more practical *Meet Tom and Sam*.

When he was finished, it didn't look bad.

Not bad at all.

Even Carl was smiling, a cinnamon bagel in his hand. His thoughts were easy to read. Call PBS now and, with your donation of $100 or more, you'll receive a DVD copy of *Meet Tom and Sam*, signed by the director.

I looked at my watch; it was just after three. A baby cried upstairs.

"You're going to love being parents," Stu said. "It really is fantastic."

"It better be," I whispered to Sam.

———————————————————

And with that, the audition was complete. No more videos to edit. No letters to write. No forms to fill out.

There would still be one home visit prior to placement. But apart from that, and checking in with Dawn periodically by phone, we had nothing to do but wait.

And wait we did.

Over the next weeks, the messages from Mom accumulated. Left unopened, they jammed my email box.

A purple dinosaur, Grace's gun-jumping gift to our baby, stared back at me each time I passed the guest room. "Oh boy, oh boy, oh boy," Barney taunted. "You might as well go ahead and get the nursery ready. Long as you have to look at me."

I bought a plastic triceratops to keep him in line.

"We're trying our best to stay positive," I told Ellen from my place on the bookstore bench. "I want to relish my last years of being spoiled and self-centered."

"There's nothing wrong with optimism," she said. "Some

things do go right, after all. Just look at your cat."

"Good point," I agreed. "Hobbes seems to be enjoying the best days of his life. Sam thinks he faked his cancer to get more treats."

"Well, it sounds like you're being sensible," she said, while parting the stacks of books on the counter. "Worrying won't lessen the wait."

"We've already met one desperate couple," I said. "We can't turn into them."

"If it ever starts getting to you, I mean really getting to you, you've got an open invitation to drop by our house. Spend some time with our real-life happy ending. You know how much Grace likes you two."

Fittingly, I took the long way home from her store, hitting the gravel trail that meandered up the mesa's side and through our suburb's greenest green space. This was a place where runoff from the reservoir benefited the grasses, trees, birds, and mosquitoes. Halfway up, a coyote crossed my path — and stopped briefly to survey me. I wanted to see this as a sign, and wished I knew more Native American lore. I imagined an Arapahoe warrior thanking Father Sky and whispering, I must treasure the things I'm about to give up. I must relish my last years of being spoiled and self-centered.

CHAPTER ELEVEN
CLOSE CALLS.

After nine months of waiting, we had already jumped to 14 on the list.

"It's been busy," Dawn warned after sharing the news. "You could be caught off guard."

Clicking off the phone, I wanted to shout and cry and dance in my chair. I wanted to surprise Sam at work with flowers and champagne, hugging her for minutes in front of stunned co-workers. "At last," I'd whisper as the others in her meeting took notes. "We're going to be parents."

At the same time, I wanted to drive to the airport, ditch my car at curbside, and hop the first flight to Tahiti, where I would take up residence in a Gauguin oil.

This was what my neighbors were doing, though in point of fact, they tended to return from their exotic escapes. "It's our turn to be selfish now," they might as well have shouted. "Our children all live far away and are gainfully employed."

Flaunting their new independence, the bastards painted their houses when the old paint was barely starting to peel. They added hot tubs and sunrooms, and paid strangers to keep their yards from looking like mine.

Once behind their newly painted walls, they accumulated stuff they didn't plan on using or even looking at much, filling their empty nests with sports memorabilia, Buns of Steel infomercial products, and trendy overpriced stereos that looked like cheap clock radios.

It should have been us with The Buns of Steel Step 2000.

But this was not to be. In our house, in my world, everything had to go. The boxes of quadraphonic tapes. The pool table "loaned" to us by Mac when the bank foreclosed on his condo. The filing cabinets molded from lead to withstand nuclear blasts.

"Mac says that when our kid's older we'll be sorry we gave up the pool table."

"We'll just have to learn to live with the loss," Sam said, while looking at my vintage poster for *London Calling*. By the Only Band That Matters. The bottom strip of its black plastic frame had come loose at one end and now tilted floorward at a sixty-degree angle.

"A little paint," she said, "and it will be nice down here."

She was referring to our plan to finally finish the basement, which, if memory served me well, had started out as her plan. Sometime during the months to come, I would relocate my office, going subterranean like those Mole People on Superman, to free up space for baby. Unlike our neighbors' home-improvement projects, this one wouldn't benefit from illegal immigrant labor. I could do it cheaper.

This last part was important. We now had a budget, the messy kind English majors draw up on the back of old manuscript pages.

The budget was waiting for us upstairs. It covered a good chunk of the kitchen table.

"All these expenses," I said as Sam grabbed a glass of water and took her place on the table's far side. "We have to balance the columns."

She questioned some of my numbers, contending it couldn't possibly cost 1.3 million dollars to enroll a kid in an unaccredited two-year college. "Even in 2019."

"Well — that's what I read," I told her, leaving off "on the Internet."

"Where did you get $400 for childproofing? Are we padding the ceilings?"

"Carl and Penny paid at least that much."

Sam pointed out that my columns were tilting, even merging in places.

Ignoring her negativity, I said, "There's diapers and daycare and clothing and—"

"What? Elocution lessons?" Sam reached across the balance sheet and took my hand. "We can afford diapers ... whatever you've been telling your readers. It'll work out. You'll see."

I wasn't so sure, not when babeebudget.com put diapers for one infant at $300 a week. No wonder the website kept urging me to immediately contact their "skilled family-investment mentors."

My wife didn't understand budgets.

We drove for two days to see Sam's dad and visit April's grave. The cats came with us, because Hobbes wasn't ready to let anyone but me shove medicine down his throat — and so I could cement my reputation as the family eccentric.

The boys proved good company in a St. Louis motel room that had obviously accommodated other pets. They hunted and posed like the stars of Walt Disney wildlife shorts as their feral instincts kicked in. They even staged one of their mock fights, Bud with his right paw in the air, ready to strike, but never quite striking. The kittens who used to tear up our D.C. townhouse had mellowed into the sweetest imaginable companions. I was lucky to know them. This was followed by another thought: Our kid would do just the opposite. No sooner would I grow used to a fresh source of loyalty and love than some purple-haired changeling would be telling me to eat poop and die.

Bud and Hobbes weren't such good company in the car, despite having the back half to themselves. Bud produced a most unmusical cry, sustaining each rusty-nail sound for stretches that would have left Dame Kiri Te Kanawa gasping for air.

After stopping for gas just east of Nashville, we thought Hobbes had escaped. Neither Sam nor I could see him ... until he crawled out from under the driver's seat to squeeze between my foot and the pedals. "For a cat who's been dead two years," Sam said as we pulled off onto the Emergency Lane, "he's still got a pretty full tank."

We were happy to arrive at Luther's house, where a meal larger than the one we'd eaten two hours before waited for us. It was just after nine.

Luther's kitchen. Luther's house. We adjust too easily, I thought, picking at my fifteen-ounce pork chop sautéed in butter. We let go too quickly of our "and April's."

One evening and several meals later, we were sitting on Luther's couch, watching the news, which provided a break from watching shows that weren't the news. The usual murders and rumblings of war had me asking, "And why is it we're so eager to perpetuate the species?"

Ironically, that very eagerness was the topic of the final report.

A woman whose tall blond hair didn't fit completely on

screen said, "These huge advances are making in vitro fertilization increasingly efficient."

A caption identified her as the head technician at Nashville's Skyline Fertility Clinic. "IVF has come of age," she said. "For millions of couples, the choice is much clearer."

She then explained why, sharing statistics better than any Webb had put forth. Though it didn't sound like the odds of conception had improved, the risk of multiple births was greatly reduced.

"Is that what y'all tried?" Luther asked.

"Almost," I said, waiting for Sam to point out that we should have held out for the huge advances.

But she surprised me, as always. "We're glad we chose adoption. In vitro would have dented our savings right when we needed them." She reached into the bowl of boiled peanuts Luther had placed on the coffee table. "But this sure is good news for everyone going that route."

Her dad tapped a cigarette free of its pack and said, "I reckon that's true."

Bud shot through the room, with Hobbes on his tail, a sight followed by the sound of glass breaking, a lamp or family heirloom. "Oh, Lord," said Sam, fixing me with a stare that asked, *Did we have to bring them both?*

Over the next few days we talked with Luther about moving to Colorado "to be near your grandchild."

And each time we did he grew defensive, saying, "I like it here."

When Luther's friend came over for dinner the last night, it was obvious she was more than a friend, especially when she said, "I want you to think of me as family."

Sam looked uneasy, as did I. Not that I had a problem with Luther finding new love. My concern was more selfish in nature. Lucille represented an ongoing relationship between me and Bristol, Tennessee. With her in Luther's life and kitchen and cigarette supply, he was much less likely to move west than before.

Still... I couldn't make assumptions.

And on that assumption I asked, "Have you ever been to Colorado?"

"Memphis," said Lucille. "Furtherest I been. We like it here."

Sam and I were barely over our car lag from the return trip when Dawn called.

"It's Saturday," I said. "We're not missing a class?"

"No, something bigger than that." We were up for consideration, she said, provided we made a tough decision. "The baby's already born. A preemie. Eighteen weeks early."

Within hours, Sam and I were authorities on the subject of premature babies, tutored by the Internet.

"Yes," we told our caseworker. "Please submit our video and letters."

It was eight o'clock before we realized we hadn't eaten. I ordered a pizza, and promptly forgot I had done so, leaving it for the delivery guy to surprise me in my pajama shorts at 8:35.

While watching our Cheese Lovers Special grow cold, we talked about naming babies and painting basements. We also talked each other down whenever one of us thought it couldn't hurt to call Luther or Mom or a number chosen randomly from the phone book, "just to tell someone."

"What are you doing?" I cried as I came out of the bathroom. "Please, honey, please, put that thing down. This is no time to get crazy."

"But—"

"We're not watching the video. It will only make us paranoid."

Sunday crawled by like a construction zone. Left Lane Closed Next Forty Miles. I caught Sam watching the video.

On Monday afternoon, I took another call. We hadn't made the cut.

I knew we didn't look fun enough.

"Don't take it personally," said Dawn. "She wanted the child to grow up in the country. Your video needed horses, not cats."

Sam disappeared, or so it seemed when she took an extra three hours to get home from work that evening. After driving high into the foothills, she parked alongside the creek that starts near Moffet Tunnel. She turned off the engine, but didn't bother undoing her seat belt and shoulder strap. Her one open window let her eavesdrop on the creek and its hundreds of garbled barroom conversations. Time passed unmeasured, at least where she was. And in the graying light, she watched a doe lead her fawn to the water. She watched rocks slide down the bank as a coal train rumbled east toward Denver and the plains.

"Want to talk?" I asked when she emerged from our garage.

She didn't.

We went through this again a few months later after backing down on another nonnegotiable condition of ours. (This birth mother wanted annual meetings with the adoptive parents and child.) Upon learning that we had not been selected to take part in those yearly reunions, Sam wanted to know, "Is this really meant to happen?"

"With these two babies," I said, "apparently not."

"I'm tired of being set up."

"Dawn said we shouldn't get discouraged."

Silence.

"Look at it from my perspective," I said. "As a writer. I've discovered a whole new world of rejection notices."

Sam's mood had worsened since Bristol. She ate little, slept poorly. This was a shame, because soon, she'd be losing sleep for an entirely new reason.

———————————————

As we neared the end of July, Sam decided it was time to tell her team at work about our secret life. Saying goodbye to yet another Sunday afternoon, she honed her announcement before a practice audience of one.

"Tom and I have been in the adoption process for close to a year," she began, looking past me as she spoke. "When we become parents, I'm taking three months for family leave. After that, I'll be working part time, four days a week. But there's no saying when this will happen. Our wait could last another year."

She paused, and I recognized my cue to assure her she was doing fine.

"We've been told things are moving fast at the agency," she resumed. "Tom believes something could happen as early as October or November."

"I think you should say, *we* believe."

"I guess that sounds better," she said. "Even if it's not true."

Hobbes ambled into the kitchen, stopping near the refrigerator door and two empty saucers. I got up to do my duty.

"Keep going," I said. "I'm listening."

"I'm going to tell them Tuesday."

"Tuesday. Good."

"Workload permitting," she added.

Her workload wouldn't get a say in the matter.

———————————————

Early that Monday, my monitor screen went dark. There was a cry from downstairs: Hobbes requesting my presence by the refrigerator door where I could be useful. It was 9:26, exactly as it was when I last checked my watch. I had yet to type an entire sentence. My eyelids kept getting in the way.

Bored as a cat on a cross-country trip, I had no idea I was enjoying my last moments of carefree bliss. No one had bothered to tell me. The phone rang and I grabbed it as I would an oxygen mask in a 747 filling with smoke. And while I was willing to talk water purification systems with the telemarketer whose mother I slandered only days before, my luck was on the rebound. It was Dawn at the adoption agency, calling to ask, "How are you two holding up?"

"Compared to what?" I said. "My father-in-law called twice this weekend to see if we had news. We should never have told anyone we were under consideration that first time."

"I didn't think you had—"

"Sam broke down and called him from work. Right before the first rejection."

Dawn commiserated, and I said, "She's planning to tell her coworkers what we've been up to."

"I think that's a good plan."

"You don't think she'll be pestered even more?"

"I think it's a good plan. There's such a thing as waiting too long and getting caught off guard." Dawn then let slip this was no routine query — and that my boredom wouldn't be returning any time soon. "I can't tell you more right now. But you might want to shop for an infant car seat."

You never fail until

you stop trying.

_____

ALBERT EINSTEIN

CHAPTER TWELVE
EXPECTANT.

On Tuesday morning we learned that a five-day-old girl was considering us as parents. The biological mother had asked for videos and letters, and the agency had given her ours, as well as those of four other couples viewed as workable matches.

Telling me this, Dawn seemed strangely optimistic for someone who had twice before ripped off our wings in the middle of flight. "The car seat?" she said. "Did you get one?"

That afternoon Sam let her coworkers into the loop... almost. As we'd both agreed, no one needed to know about recent developments. We didn't want more condolences when baby went home with someone else. "As early as October or November" remained the official line.

Buoyed by the support she received, Sam was happy when she got home. "They couldn't have been more thrilled or surprised. Anything new from Dawn?"

On Wednesday afternoon, the phones stopped ringing altogether, which finally prompted me to pick one up and — son of a bitch, today of all days — find out it was dead. I could only assume one thing: After trying to call me a few dozen times, Dawn gave up and called Sam at work. My wife then tried calling me four dozen times before going to meet the birth mother on her own and pick up the baby — the baby that would never bond with me because of this debacle. Sam and her daughter would hate me for the rest of my life, almost as much as I'd hate our ex-service provider.

At 4:17, the phone in my office announced it was working again. Dawn was calling... for the first time that day. I had not missed any important developments.

"I'm still feeling good about this one," she confided. "Like I keep saying, you should be prepared."

I wanted to hear her elaborate, specifically by saying, "The other couples' videos are crap." But the words never came.

Come noon the next day, no decision had been reached; it didn't seem to matter how many times Sam and I bugged our caseworker. All Dawn could say was, "Hold tight," or "Be patient."

Just before five, Dawn called to say, "I shouldn't tell you this, but I know you're going crazy with waiting. It looks like she made up her mind. She just needs to be sure."

A few seconds later: "Tom? Tom..."

"Well," I said. "This is no ordinary extraordinary occurrence." I asked a few questions about the birth mother, but apart from telling me that she was in her mid-twenties, Dawn withheld details.

"We must not have looked *that* ancient to her," I said.

"From what I've been told, you were her choice from the start."

"She could back out."

"You have to trust me," Dawn said. "It's looking good. Very good."

Needless to say, these words inspired more caution than optimism. Sam and I had heard them before.

He that can have patience

can have what he will.

_____

BENJAMIN FRANKLIN

CHAPTER THIRTEEN

POSITIVE RESULTS.

Here was something new: "You meet the birth mother on Monday, and if things work out, you'll meet your daughter that afternoon."

Adopting one child won't

change the world;

but for that child,

the world will change.

_____

UNKNOWN

CHAPTER FOURTEEN

INSTANT BABY. JUST ADD MILK.

After all the warnings that we might be caught off guard, we were caught off guard. As for having what we needed to bring a baby home — car seats, diapers, formula, and so on — we had the home. And even then, all the rooms were in the wrong places. The guest room bed still dominated the nursery, while my computer and desk continued their occupation of the guest room, refusing to yield to the bed.

My office, as you know, had been promised new digs in the basement. But the basement wasn't quite ready. And so we spent most of our last child-free weekend painting drywall and trim, lighting the first stick of dynamite to break the furniture logjam. In between coats, we ventured out to our local *Big Box Baby Store*, where we purchased the top-rated car seat, then drove into Boulder to borrow a bassinet. At night, we practiced going without sleep, just as we'd been doing since Dawn first called. So much to remember, so much to get done. The hailstorm of thought would not let up.

It was five o'clock Sunday when I realized that while the basement looked great, the car seat still sat in its crate. "One more thing I'd better do," I grumbled while rinsing my paint-brush in the kitchen sink. "A cardboard box with holes in the top is not going to impress Dawn."

Sam asked if I needed her help.

"I don't know. I left three messages with the state patrol."

"State patrol?"

"They install these things — or claim to."

"You could ask a neighbor."

"In a perfect world, I'd do just that. But no one seems to be home this weekend."

As if on cue, the phone rang and Trooper Steve introduced himself. "Understand you need an assist."

"Yes," I said, "but I've run out of time. We have to be in south Denver tomorrow." We were due at our agency at half-past ten, giving Dawn a scant thirty minutes to prepare us for the second most important meeting of our married lives: birth mother at eleven. It took an hour to get there at speeds not recommended by the state patrol, and I was hoping to shower and dress before leaving, going those extra inches to impress the birth mother and her caseworker, both of whom still had the power to reject us. "Any chance we could stop en route?" I asked Trooper Steve. "Say, in the spare seconds between 8:45 and 8:46?"

He laughed and said, "We deliver. Provided there aren't any fatals between now and then, I could be there by six."

And so it was still light outside when Sam first asked a uniformed state trooper if it was okay to take his photo while he buckled the car-seat base into position.

"No problemo," he replied, and we learned that Steve was a new dad himself — eight weeks in. "I like doing this," he added. "I don't like working fatals, especially when they involve small children and could have been prevented."

I was amazed by the amount of force required to make the base an immovable object. Mustering all available body weight, Steve pressed down on the uneven plastic surface with his knee. I could tell this was painful, even if Steve wasn't the kind of state trooper who cried in front of strangers. He then tugged at the belt with his last reserves of strength, his face turning red, knee still in harm's way.

"Got it?" he asked before baffling us by releasing the seat belt and backing out of the car, taking the base with him.

Sam fairly shouted, "Isn't that supposed to hold the seat in place?"

"I want each of you to take a turn at installing the base."

"It looked painful," I said.

"You'll need to know this."

I went first, and quickly learned that, agreeable as Steve was, having a state trooper watch me perform a task does not bring out my agility and strength. "You should use this as part of your sobriety test," I suggested as the seat belt twisted in the wrong direction.

"Concentrate," he said, and I wanted to ask, *On what? The prospect of going through life with one good knee?* "You're not pressing down hard enough."

"Sorry... sorry," I muttered under my breath, "I'm having a problemo."

Sam secured it in half the time. "Nice job," Steve told her. "It's good to see a responsible parent."

———————————

I was clean and fully dressed the following morning when we met Laura, the strong, selfless woman who wanted her biological child to know things she couldn't teach her. "I've never seen the ocean," she said as her caseworker motioned for us to take seats in a tight circle of folding chairs. "I've got so many dreams that won't ever happen. I want them to happen for her."

One thing helped to put me at ease, to the extent it was possible. Laura reminded me of a Denver friend — a feisty Texas transplant who worked in the music business, repping for Warner's. Laura could have been Jamie's sister, in fact, united by spunk and some physical similarities, had it not been for that ex-Tex factor. Our birth mother had grown up on Colorado's eastern plains.

Laura revealed another dream, saying, "I didn't stick it out in school. I don't want this to be true for—" She paused before using the name we had chosen. "Evelyn."

I assured her we'd do our best to make Evelyn hunger for knowledge. Sam went one step further, telling Laura, "It's never too late to go back to school. I'm speaking from experience."

The office belonged to Laura's caseworker. We recognized Rachel from our second education class, where she'd been one of the speakers. Rachel had looked different then in that she wasn't pregnant. This was why Dawn had reintroduced her as "the world's most conscientious caseworker. Rachel stops at nothing to create a bond with her clients."

The meeting was emotional, for us, for Dawn, for Laura and Rachel. But we also laughed — all five of us — and I took this as a good sign. Rachel asked if we were ready to keep our unwritten agreement with the birth mother to send photos and progress reports at six-month intervals through the agency. "That was always the plan," I said, and Sam asked if Laura wouldn't mind providing a photo of herself at some point in the future. "For Evelyn."

On the drive down, Sam had told me she wanted to ask why we'd been selected. "You could be sorry," I said. "Remember Dawn's story about the couple that was chosen because a pregnant eighteen-year-old saw a couch in their video that reminded her 'of the one in Mom's house'?"

I didn't bring up the more common response that older couples received, "He reminds me of my dad."

Sam risked humility. Looking into Laura's eyes, she asked, "Would you be comfortable sharing why you picked us?"

Laura didn't hesitate. "He's funny," she said.

But as much as I like repeating this exchange, her answer was funny in itself in that I couldn't remember being anything but nervous when we shot our video and wrote the letters. Still, her words offered proof that Evelyn was meant to be with us — and grow up to be a smartass like her old man. They also reinforced my belief that a sense of humor is essential to surviving infertility.

"I liked that he works at home," she said next. "I liked that he'll spend time with her." This surprised me as well in that I'd been expecting my lack of a commute to cost us points. In the sample videos Sam and I had watched, the wives all made the very same promise, as if reading from a standardized script: "I plan to retire and never lift a finger outside of our lovely home unless lifting that finger will affect our child's development in a positive manner."

"One more thing," Laura said. "The cats. That showed you could take care of others."

I couldn't have found a better place to insert my joke: *That reminds me, will she need her own litter box?* But Sam hadn't laughed when I tested it on friends, and so, with great effort, I held my peace.

Ironically, however, it was Sam who misspoke and got the puzzled looks. Her response to Laura's perfectly sound reasons for choosing us — "Tom was afraid you'd say it was our couch" — simply baffled the other women. Needless to say, I had no choice but to bail out my wife with the litter-box joke.

Laura talked about her childhood in rural Colorado, explaining how her older brothers trained the family goat to pin her to the barn with its horns. She told us why she chose adoption, then gave us two photos. "Oh, Evelyn," I whispered, taking in my daughter. Hours old at the time, she was wide-eyed and shaggy on top, with one roller-coaster curl that brought to mind Bob's Big Boy.

"She's gorgeous," Sam said, and it was true.

"She is," Laura whispered, and while I heard more pride than sadness, the latter was hardly inaudible. Sam and I kept our eyes on the photos.

"Questions?" Rachel stepped in, sensing that the meeting was over. "Anyone?"

We rose from our chairs to exchange friendly hugs, and Sam said, "I hope you realize your dreams." Her hand rested on Laura's forearm. "I hope you see the ocean."

Sam and I were barely inside Dawn's office when I blurted, "Let's do it."

"Agreed," Sam said. "This is the one."

"You'll get no argument from me," Dawn said, taking her seat and glancing at some papers on the desk, "but we're still waiting to make sure Laura's okay with her initial decision."

She asked Sam to pull the door, but this proved impossible. Rachel was standing in it. "So—" She was smiling as well. "It's good on our end. All I need are some willing adoptive parents. What have you got for me, Dawn?"

I heard a long "Thank God" while Sam grabbed my hand and attempted to crush it. "I'm already in love with that baby and we haven't even met her."

"I take it that's a yes," Rachel said.

We told the caseworkers how lucky we felt. We liked the

birth mother. She seemed to be an intrinsically decent, intelligent person who had endured bad breaks and, like everyone else negotiating a passage through this life, a few bad decisions. She clearly wanted the best for Evelyn.

"Before today," Sam said, finally freeing my hand from her trash-compactor grip, "I worried about things we'd have to tell our child. That was the one part of adoption that scared me to death. Those serious talks when she's a teen." I knew exactly what Sam was saying. As adoptive parents, it would be our duty to share our child's birth history, all of it, however dark or potentially damaging. In eighteen years, she would see it on her own — the law made this clear — and the surest way to nurture mistrust was to withhold information.

"Now," Sam continued, "I don't think it will be that hard. Laura's a good person, and she told us more about the birth father than we ever thought we'd know. It just wasn't the right time for either of them to raise a child."

"That's been our opinion," said Rachel.

"Speaking of Laura—" Dawn interrupted.

"Yeah, I know. She must be wondering what happened to me."

"We're going to meet with her one more time," Dawn explained. "Are we ready? Mom? Dad?"

Sam grabbed a fresh tissue from the box on Dawn's desk.

"Almost forgot," Rachel said, stopping just outside the door. "You need to know she won't be at the Placement Ceremony tomorrow, when this all becomes official. She said her good-byes at the hospital — that's how she feels. I think she knows just what she can bear."

This made even more sense when we returned to Rachel's office. Laura had changed, though the word I really wanted was, *diminished.* Like the moon at that instant the fog first rolls in, she seemed distant and pale. One look at my wife explained this phenomenon, for she had changed too. Sam was aglow, no fog factor here. The aura of motherhood, so tangible at that moment, had clearly been passed from one woman to another.

Despite my concern for Laura, I couldn't help but wonder if I, too, looked different. Did dads metamorphose? It only seemed fair. Certainly, I was hosting emotions that were new to me, or new in this concentration. I doubted I was radiating, however.

Rachel broke the silence that had gone unnoticed by the rest of us. "This child is going to have an extraordinary life. I know it." She faced Laura as she spoke. "And she'll have you to thank. For what you're doing today."

Dawn waited a few seconds before asking, "Anything else? This is the time to speak up."

"There is one thing," Sam said, reaching into a small shopping bag for the silver pendant heart purchased that morning at Tiffany's. This was among the least expensive items in their Denver store, but still outside of our budget. It had also been out of our way, adding twenty minutes to the morning's drive.

After watching what came next, I was glad Sam had suggested the detour. "This is nothing compared to what you're giving us," my beautiful wife said quietly as she handed the gift box to Laura. "We want this to remind you that we'll always hold you in our hearts."

Laura opened her present and beamed, tearfully. Her "Thanks" came out as a sigh, and it was clear that we were facing a woman who had never been in Tiffany's, though in truth, this was one thing she'd held in common with me right up until ten o'clock that morning. Later, we learned that Laura showed her small treasure to nearly everyone at our agency. "I'm so glad I chose them," she told the director. "They were just like in their video."

Heading back north on I-25, Sam revealed she had something special planned for that evening. "I picked up champagne. If you wouldn't mind grilling some Portobello mushrooms, I'll prepare everything else. It could be our last romantic meal for a while."

This sounded good, now that we understood Evelyn wouldn't be going home with us till after Tuesday's Placement Ceremony. Though I hadn't thought to ask, I wondered why this was. Were they giving us a chance to back out if we weren't sure?

Our destination was an address in Longmont, about 30 minutes on the far side of our suburb. A cradle-care family had been watching over Evelyn. They had three kids of their own, all adopted from our agency. Dawn was meeting us there.

"We could make one stop," Sam suggested as we passed the Denver skyline. "We've got plenty of time, and we're going to need a changing table."

"Let me guess. Babies 'R' Bucks."

"It should only take a minute. Remember the one we looked at?"

"Not really. What happened to lunch?"

"Table's more important," Sam said. "Besides, I don't think I can eat right now."

"I have to admit I enjoyed our first side trip today."

"To Tiffany's? You did?"

"Did you notice how the gold sales staff worked on a higher plane than the silver people?" The store had been divided into two large showrooms, and we had to walk past the much more expensive gold and diamond items to reach our counter. "That first guy might as well have said, 'Silver? Next room. But hurry. I can't be seen talking with you.'"

"Did anyone ever tell you you're goofy?" Sam said with a laugh.

"I seem to recall 'funny,'" I said. "But goofy ... no, it's not ringing a bell."

"The Tiffany's people seemed fine to me."

"Tell you what," I said. "We can do the baby store if I'm allowed to make one more stop. Ellen's bookstore. She's got something else we'll need tomorrow."

———————————

The floor-model changing table failed to stir any memories, but standing before it, one thing became clear. This was no table. This was a split-level dresser the size of a sedan. "She really needs this for changing diapers?" I asked.

Assembly required, warned the wide box that followed us into the parking lot. And even then, it failed to mention, *All parts made of Superheavytonium. Do not lift. Do not even try.* While a store employee watched in amusement, the baby seat came out of the car, base and all, to make room for our new purchase.

"Good thing Trooper Steve had us install it on our own," Sam said.

"And tonight," I told her, "it's your turn again. I hope you've been keeping your knee in shape."

"You really are goofy," she said. "So, what's at Ellen's bookstore?"

———————————

One hour, two stops, and thirty miles later, everything changed forever. Sam and I met Evelyn.

The cutest baby we'd ever seen, she was tiny and trusting, hairy too, exactly as captured in Laura's photos. We had just been welcomed into the home of strangers, though these were not strangers to Evelyn. Karyn and Chuck, the cradle-care parents, had fed and bathed her for most of her short life. To this fragile being, Sam and I were the strangers.

Karyn held the baby.

"So what do you think?" asked Dawn from an armchair in the corner, a toy carousel-horse at her feet.

"You do good work," I said.

Taking my first real look around the living room, I noted that Karyn and Chuck were minimalists when it came to home décor. Essential furniture only, a few family photos in simple frames. I saw no museum prints, no exotic souvenirs from Bali or Spain or even the Ozarks. I knew the reason: adoption times three.

I noticed one more detail. The owners of this house appeared to be happy. Same explanation. They joked about keeping Evelyn, "making it an even four." Sam didn't laugh.

"I know they say all babies are beautiful," Dawn said, "but in my professional capacity, I can assure you it's not true. This baby ... is beautiful."

"Evelyn's been a delight," said Karyn, while handing Sam her infant daughter for the first time.

"Except at night," a boy's voice interjected from the kitchen. "She's got the room right next to mine."

The baby looked up at my wife with innocent eyes that said, "He must be mistaking me for someone else."

Sam cried, and I realized I was viewing this scene through my own tears. "Baby girl," I whispered, leaning forward. Our daughter smelled like lilacs. "Meet Mommy and Daddy."

I spent that evening eating slices of leftover pizza, stuck behind prescription reading glasses that limit my field of vision to a ten-inch radius, straining to master the *Gray's Anatomy* of instruction booklets. Dozens of parts, some dinky, some huge, concealed the guest room carpet. These in turn were encircled by hundreds of screws and bolts. "You're sure she really needs this?"

"Have some more champagne," Sam said.

"Right. Our last romantic dinner."

The following morning, we were back at the cradle-care house for the Placement Ceremony, which, impossibly, proved more emotional than anything before. As Dawn showed up with Margaret, the agency's founder, I was trying to balance a camcorder on its tripod, which now blocked the doorway that led to the dining room. Sam had borrowed this camera the night before — dashing over to Carl and Penny's while I stared down my furniture parts — and playing with it now, I couldn't tell which switch was which. But before I could dig out my glasses and remind everyone just how old I really was, Chuck the cradle-care dad came to my rescue, saying, "We've got one of those." He promptly bolted the camera into place and aimed it at the couch where Sam and I would be sitting. He also killed the Auto-Focus — something I wouldn't discover till I copied the recording — ensuring that the entire ceremony would be preserved in a washed-out blur. This was appropriate, I would later concede, since that watery distortion added realism to our record of a tear-filled affair.

Then we were ready, everyone in place. Sam and I were joined at the hip as we shared the joy of holding our baby. Evelyn seemed to stare at our faces, though I knew she relied more on hearing and smell to establish who we were.

Margaret explained how the ceremony would proceed. "As you know, each of us will have the opportunity to speak." The founder, it was clear, preferred keeping her rituals organized. "On the first go round, you may say whatever you want, provided it relates to the proceedings. Chuck, let's start with you."

"It's a privilege to watch this." The cradle-care dad had

temporarily abandoned his place behind the camera – and stood now on our blurry side. This was how we'd remember Chuck: backside only, out of focus. "We're honored to play a role in this life-changing event."

Keeping her eyes on baby Evelyn, Karyn smiled broadly and said, "Really, it was our pleasure to help her through her first days on Earth. This child is a joy. You three will have so much fun."

When it was Sam's turn to speak, she read a short poem of a prayer that Jane had left for us at the bookstore, taken from some goddess-heavy pre-Christian European religion. "Divine Mother, Giver of Life, we thank you for this precious life that has been given to us to tend and nourish." The cradle-care parents and agency professionals listened respectfully. No *Stop, stop, adoption over! This baby will not be raised by pagans!* "May your blessings follow this young one throughout her life, may she grow in beauty and wisdom, may she learn your ways and know the wonder of your creation, O great pre-Christian goddess."

"Tom," said Margaret, "do you have something you wish to contribute?"

I returned Evelyn to my wife's ready arms and, along with my glasses, pulled out the used paperback we'd picked up at Ellen's store. *Roots* by Alex Haley. Opening it to the page I had earmarked, I haltingly read the famous passage that brought to life a centuries-old naming ritual. I paraphrased extensively — the reason for my stop-and-start delivery — amending the gender to suit little Evelyn. While the others watched from a distance, I stood at the outermost edge of my village. It was long past nightfall and the sky was silky and cloudless as I lifted my baby to face the infinite expanse of stars. A cricket chirped, I adjusted my glasses. And speaking softly in deference to any noble ancestors who might be present, I instructed my daughter to "behold the only thing greater than yourself."

"All right," Margaret said. "We complete the Placement Ceremony by going around the circle one last time. Everyone is to make a wish for young Evelyn's future. Mine is that each day deliver some new joy, knowledge, and surprise."

"Am I next?" Karyn asked. "My wish for Evelyn is for her to bring as much joy to others as she's brought to us."

Our baby cried for the first time in our presence, but it lasted only seconds. For the rest of the ceremony, Sam held Evelyn close to her chest, bobbing her gently.

"You're a natural," said Chuck at the start of his turn, this time off-camera. "I wish for the three of you to have a wonderful life together."

"I wish," Dawn said with a sniffle, "for Evelyn to fulfill her potential. That she'll be as smart and happy and talented as she is capable of being."

Margaret looked at me and smiled. "Tom?"

"My biggest wish is for Evelyn to become a good person, decent and thoughtful and caring. But I also want her to find the rewards she seeks. And I want her to sleep straight through the night by the time she's three months old."

"That's aiming high," Margaret said. "Sam, do you have anything realistic to add?"

Using her free hand to wipe away tears, Sam replied, "I just want to say one thing. This was meant to be. I know it sounds strange, but I'm glad everything else went wrong."

"Your wish?" Margaret said.

"I hope we can make her as happy as she's made us today."

That first evening in our house, I watched Sam jump each time her baby breathed. I watched Bud and Hobbes dart away to seek safe haven in the basement. I watched powder and water merge to become formula in a half-gallon pitcher, watched diapers go from white to green. And I stared blankly at the bolts and screws and pressboard panels that seemed to have proliferated since the night before, where the guest room carpet used to be.

I gave up on the changing table around eleven after waking with a start, a dozen screws embedded sideways in my cheek. Shaking them loose, I stumbled across the hallway to our bedroom, determined to sleep in a hardware-free environment. But once in bed, I stayed up listening to the bubbly sounds that spilled out of the bassinet near Sam's side of the bed.

This is it. The long-delayed test. After six years of wondering how I'd react to having a helpless new being in my life, house, and ears, there she was, theory made flesh. After six years of asking how I'd really do as the father of an infant, there I was, pleasantly surprised by the answer.

Sam took my hand and whispered, "Our instant baby."

"Only took six years."

"Six years of waiting," she said. "And trying. And hoping for this moment."

"Of battling modest foes like nature, society, and the insurance industry."

I heard her sigh. "This has been the most wonderful day of my life. Did you get the changing table done?"

On Wednesday morning, our phone rang for the first of 2,000 times. "So how is it?" Ellen asked.

"We're so lucky. Perfect baby. Perfect circumstances. The birth father even showed up. He called the agency, agreeing that this was the best thing for Evelyn. He's going in Thursday to sign the relinquishment papers."

"That's wonderful," Ellen said.

"Like I said, we got lucky."

"I think you two were due some luck."

"I know this makes me a freak," I said, "but I'm still not sorry we waited as long as we did. You should see this baby. She's amazing."

Ellen told me that she, Grace, and Jane were dying to meet Evelyn, but they wanted to give us some time to catch up on our breathing. "You're going to need it. Believe me."

The luck theory was reinforced when Carl and Penny showed up that evening to welcome their new neighbor, bearing enough food to sustain a pair of grownups for several days. "And you can hold onto the camcorder for as long as you need it," Carl told us. "Within reason, of course."

"Thanks," I said. "If you could just show me the Auto-Focus."

Then the surprise — from Penny, who apparently didn't think we'd had enough surprises that week. She asked if she could speak with us, "alone," and Carl went outside, saying he'd left something back at the house. "Oh, he knows," Penny said. "I just felt this would be easier if he wasn't here."

She took a deep breath, looking down at the floor, then shyly raised her eyes to meet Sam's. "Our kids don't even know what I'm about to tell you. When I was in high school—" The portable swamp cooler whirred to life in the next room. "It happened to me. I saw adoption from the other side." Another pause. "It was the toughest thing I've ever been through, but there wasn't much of a choice. My folks made it clear I wasn't raising a child under their roof. Looking back now, I don't know how much of it was my little town in Nebraska and how much of it was the times, but things were so different. Counseling? Openness? I tell you, for those eight months

I was a non-entity.

"In the years since, you wouldn't believe how much time I've spent wondering what happened to that baby ... a baby I held for all of a minute. Still, strange as it sounds, I've always had mixed feelings about her looking for me."

Sam reached for her box of Kleenex, and handed it to Penny.

"I want to know how her life turned out," our friend resumed. "Carl would be okay with it, with her calling to say she found me. At the same time, a bigger part of me wants to keep the past where it belongs, in the past." There was the slightest hint of a smile. "I know, I know, I'm living proof that that's impossible. Anyway, what I wanted to say was ... I think ... I think that watching the two of you go through all this was what I always needed, without knowing it of course. Ever since you told us you were adopting, I've imagined you as the parents who took that baby home and made her their own. That gave me a picture, a picture I was comfortable with. It's such a big help to finally see just how much that child was wanted. More than any other child could be. These past few days, everything came full circle for me."

Sam looked over at me, and I knew what she was asking: *Could you get that other box of Kleenex from the kitchen?*

"You know, more than anything, I would've liked to meet the couple that ended up with her. Now, in some ways, it feels like I have."

The swamp cooler reached the end of its cycle, and silence settled everywhere. This was broken by Carl's light knock. Walking back in, he carried a gift, a handcrafted Kachina doll.

Penny smiled at her husband, but kept hugging Sam. "There's one thing you two need to understand. I don't regret helping that child find a better path, and someday soon, Evelyn's birth mother will feel the same way. I couldn't have lived that other life. It wouldn't have been fair. To me or that child. We both deserved better."

When this new stretch of silence threatened to last forever, Carl said, "Hey, Tom, let me show you that thing on the camera."

———————————————

On Thursday morning, I went online for the first time in days. And while deleting 800 new Spam decoys — *Increase your size and cut mortgage payments while Ukrainian farm girls clean your septic tank* — I saw the message from my mother tagged "ATTN: MOM AND DAD."

CONGRATULATIONS! BETTER LATE THAN
NEVER. TELL MY GRANDCHILD, EVELYN,
I LOVE HER AND CAN'T WAIT TO SEE HER.
XXXXXXOOOOOOO GRANDMA.

That afternoon, Dawn called to report that the birth father had stayed true to his word and relinquished his rights. The bottle of champagne came back out, and from a blanket on the floor, Evelyn did her best to watch as I fastened the handles to the changing table drawers, which were still arranged in pieces about the room. The main frame now stood as a single solid unit, though five empty tunnels cried out for me to complete those drawers.

That happened on Friday. By the time Evelyn dozed off for her first short nap, only six screws remained of the original 2,796. My wrist ached from carpal tunnel — newly acquired, I plan to sue — as I turned a page in the instruction booklet to find there were no more steps, only a dubious 100% Total Satisfaction Guarantee. *Simply disassemble the item and return by Priority Mail in its original packaging...* I looked to my left and, sure enough, saw a changing table identical to the one in the storeroom display.

Sporting the giddy smile of a new dad who had finished a glass of champagne after barely sleeping for days on end, I pulled myself up from the floor. The last of my joints snapped back into place, and I lumbered across the hall. "What's going on?" Sam asked as I removed Evelyn from her bassinet. "You know she's going to cry."

"Silence. You must follow."

Then the three of us huddled in the room that had just taken its first real step toward becoming a nursery. "Incredible," Sam said. "It's just like the floor model. Except for ... the handles, are they right side up?"

Without responding, I held my daughter out before me, my hands on her sides, tucked beneath her armpits. She was facing the changing table. She looked tiny before it.

"Sweet baby Evelyn," I said, "behold the only thing greater than yourself."

A baby is an inestimable

blessing and bother.

_____

MARK TWAIN

CHAPTER FIFTEEN

THE GREEN BADGE OF COURAGE.

Sirens wail — we're under siege. It's 3 a.m. My commander is shouting, *"LaMarr, move out!"*

Fumbling in the darkness, I find a fresh diaper but can't force open the plastic container of baby wipes. My hands shake; Sam's opinion to the contrary, I need a Diet Pepsi. My caffeine-to-blood ratio has slipped back in favor of that useless red stuff. *"Now, old man, go!"*

This is life during wartime: no sympathy, no sleep. I'm staring into the bowels of hell — or perhaps more accurately, the bowels from hell, since baby erupts every few hours. I've never witnessed anything like this before, and as the personal assistant to two cats, I've cleaned my share of litter boxes, if not with the cats still in them. When this foe produces mustard gas, there's mustard to go with it, and she's capable of launching a volley clear across the changing table and onto the walls and floor. I'm tempted to take the clean diaper and press it to my face, to shield myself from the odors and sights as I stand here alone, begging for sleep or a merciful death, while a crescent-moon night light throws shadows across a plush toy elephant that didn't look so sinister by day.

The enemy is wily. Seven pounds light and cute as, well, a baby, she holds tactical superiority in that she weakens us with love. The daughter we waited six years to meet — the daughter we've known for all of three days — seems determined to bring us down.

Age, too, works in her favor. Evelyn senses that the old man is losing a larger war to atrophy, that his neck burns, his vision blurs, and his arms fall asleep before she does when he rocks her. Compared to my bone-dry reserves, her energy is boundless, as is her stockpile of smelly green muck. "Baby girl," I whisper, "can't you see I'm too old for this?"

The toxic diaper is peeled away, and I treat it with all the respect due a live grenade as I lurch through a minefield of musical toys and yellowing burp rags. My target is a biohazard pail marketed under the name, Diaper Genie. I lift the lid, and the squishy white ball drops silently into a plastic liner designed to eliminate odors. Snapping the lid back into place, I congratulate myself on my steadiness in battle.

Next up in my sleep-deprived fantasy, the President of the United States is holding out a Purple Heart and wondering where to pin it on the frayed tank-top shirt that's become, along with a pair of pajama shorts, my standard combat gear. The Commander-in-Chief wipes a tear from her eye (hey, as long as I'm dreaming) and says, "It's moments like these make my job worthwhile."

But what I'm looking at now is a purple head. Baby's unhappy and won't tell me why. With a dab of ointment on my finger, I wax and buff till her bottom shines. Soon the new diaper is firmly in place, soft and warm against her flesh, and I wish I were big enough to say, "I'm glad one of us is comfortable," without being sarcastic as I lift my wailing daughter from the changing table. That sarcasm, of course, will come back to haunt me when she's seventeen and seeing a psychiatrist, but I don't have the strength to care. It's 3:46 in the morning and I'm searching for a way to wash my hands without interrupting the rocking motion that calms her in theory, and without further straining a back that was already in need of a morphine drip before I bent over this last time to pick her up. So why is she the one who's crying?

"Hush, little baby. Hush."

It's then I receive my real-life reward. Sam slips into the room and says, "I think she's hungry. That's why she's crying." It gets better. "I warmed a bottle for you. Here."

Then I'm sitting in our La-Z-Boy rocker, baby cradled in my arm, time at a standstill. The war and all its metaphors seem as distant as smoke on the horizon, as I look up through slanted blinds at a hazy crescent moon that seems eerily familiar.

In an instant, the night is transformed, along with the room. The ceiling and walls are gone, and a trillion stars shine as if they never heard of pollution. We're on an African plain, I realize, just me and my daughter and a La-Z-Boy chair. Two wildcats stare from a distance, but I sense no danger. Something in their eyes gives them away. These guys are as harmless as housecats. Our housecats.

Everything here is primal: Evelyn's hunger, her trust, my feeling connected to a thousand distant ancestors. The calm is profound, as deep as the dark sky. I'll pay for this tomorrow, I know. I also know it's worth it.

I know, too, that I am crying, just as I did when I first met Evelyn. "Mmh, mmh, mmh," she sputters, draining the bottle. Baby was hungry. She's happy now.

Back in bed, my mind behaves strangely. It's teaching me something new about imprinting, specifically that the process works both ways. The cells in my brain are absorbing my daughter, taking her in as a permanent, prevalent part of their makeup. While falling asleep, I see her face, really see her face. The apparition hovers before me, letting me memorize the contours and shapes, the shadows of her mouth and eyes, the softness and roundness. If I start to roll over or reposition my arm, she's there in ghost form, blocking my way. When my eyes reopen, the face is still there.

Of course, the reason my eyes reopen is that I hear her very real screaming. "Your turn, honey," I mumble, and though off-duty, I know I'm up to stay. Sam whisks baby across the hall to the changing table, closing both doors behind her as they vanish. But forty hardwood doors sealed shut with railroad spikes and Superglue wouldn't muffle baby's outburst, and the sounds she makes tear through me like shrapnel. A battlefield flashback: I'm on the frontline, one misstep shy of hell, a premium super-absorbent diaper with smiling purple dinosaurs on the waistband pressed against my face.

Evelyn returns in one of her good moods. She's talking and singing, doing her best to tell the world, "I'm here and ready to play." Even after she falls asleep, Evelyn tests her vocal limits. Monkeys chatter and horses whinny. She mimics an alley cat in heat that's been sucking helium between musical offerings, and my wife responds with laughter. "We've adopted Yoko Ono," she whispers.

I know what Evelyn's really doing, and singing's only part of it. Like me, she's imprinting. She's seeing our faces, the shapes at least, staring back from the void of night. She's taking them in, along with the odors of our breath and bodies, the texture of our hair. *Bonded*, I think. *You're stuck with us now, baby.*

Whenever Evelyn's quiet, Sam leans over to check on her. In nine minutes, she does this nine times. "You should see your daughter," Sam says. "She looks like a little angel."

"Yes," I concur without getting up, "a sweet little screaming, farting, pooping angel."

At last, I'm feeling drowsy. One tiny ripple in a vast, vast sea. The old man is sleeping... and dreaming of his daughter's face.

Days aren't much easier on new middle-aged parents. Between runs to the drug store — "She needs more what?" — and trying to find the cats to beg forgiveness for putting formula in their dishes, we're fighting the effects of sleep deprivation. We forget to lock doors, water plants, and feed ourselves. We find it impossible to both run upstairs and remember the reason we ran upstairs.

But if the absence of REM sleep is truly the culprit, where does being older figure into this? Obviously, parents in their twenties have to deal with lack of sleep, but since they were never used to 9:30 bedtimes, they're simply swapping Conan O'Brien for changing diapers. Hardly the stuff of Purple Hearts. We, on the other hand, are looking pretty ragged. Our friends advise, "You've got to nap when baby naps." This, unfortunately, is shorthand for "Nap, eat, shave, bathe, watch ten minutes of a movie, write this damn book, try to have sex, and brush your teeth when baby naps."

Then there's the matter of middle-aged body parts, all of which are in need of replacement. My liver shows signs of acetaminophen poisoning, and when baby screams, "Pick me up," my joints refuse to bend at the proper angles. "I'm feeling my age and then some," I concede to Sam while standing before the kitchen counter, trying to determine just how many spoonfuls of soggy cornflakes I can gulp down before a relative phones, a neighbor knocks, or baby cries down the stairs for room service.

Sam responds by showing me her compassionate side: "Do you have to lie on your back and snore?" As it turns out, she's angry because I allegedly slept three hours during the night just ended. Her resentment is justified, I learn, since she racked up only two golden hours of slumber.

She's forgetting who the enemy is. She's taking sides with the cuter, smaller combatant, and I'm supposed to understand. (It's called maternal instinct, after all, not informed maternal preference.) But as much as I want to empathize, I've only had three hours of sleep myself, and so I respond, "Can't you see you're complaining to the wrong person? In sixteen years of marriage, I've yet to ask you to change my diaper or fetch me warm milk. And I only cry in bed at appropriate times."

Days pass, I can't say how many. Time is measured in feedings now, and it slows to an arthritic crawl while baby's bottle warms in a plastic *Crouching Tiger, Hidden Dragon* souvenir cup. This process takes only four minutes, but she's quick to point out that anything more than a minute represents a good chunk of her life. Her face turns red, as red as the lungs I'm viewing through the cavernous hole her sweet little mouth has somehow turned into. *Evil spirit, leave this body. Out, thee, in the name of our Father!*

But my reward always comes with the ding of the timer. Evelyn shows me her tender side, letting me see just how happy she is when the rubber nipple meets her lips and she finally tastes the soy-based formula that smells like my tattered old tennis shoes right after I mow the lawn. Her eyes try to focus on the ones I'm trying to focus, and if she could speak I know she would say, "Thanks, Dad, that was more than worth the wait. I'm sorry I behaved inappropriately." Not that I would hear these words, having developed tinnitus during her caterwaul, which lasted the same number of seconds — two hundred and forty — as it registered in decibels.

Fortunately, I don't need my hearing. I'm feeling the breeze on an African plain, watching gazelles as they pass, unmindful of our presence. The sun should be blazing, but opts instead for gently soothing. Evelyn stares in my direction. I wonder what she sees.

I know she can hear me whisper the words, "I love you, baby girl."

Just before I collide with my mattress, I catch sight of myself in the mirror. Geezer Dad in freefall. It hits me that I'm about 1,000 times older than the girl in the bassinet. One thousand times. This ratio will improve as time goes by, of course. But I'd have to live a long, long time, well past the average LaMarr family expectancy, to be only double her age. There's even less likelihood of us both surviving another 800 or 900 years, a feat that would render negligible the gap between birth dates.

"The good news," I whisper to Sam, "is that while my body's falling apart, my mind seems to be functioning properly. As most any zoologist will tell you, the mammalian brain has been programmed for eons to function without sleep and physical gratification of any sort while caring for a baby. But here's the big find, the one that belongs in textbooks: This encoding doesn't break down as we age. It's not a case of use it or lose it. Before Evelyn, there was no way I could have survived on crumbs of sleep. Yet here I am, not only marginally functioning, but also caring for a new life — and doing a damn good job of the latter.

"It's really quite amazing, don't you think?"

No response, from bassinet or bed. Everyone else is sleeping. It is amazing.

More days pass, and to my great delight I'm only 500 times older than Evelyn. It feels like she's been here forever — a comment that can be taken in both good and bad ways. The house smells like baby, every room, every inch. This puzzles the cats, and earns their displeasure. Before baby, odors were their responsibility. The cats want her out. I buy them off with tuna.

There are positive developments. Our daughter sleeps longer and defecates less. And while she still coos and yaps and Yoko Onos while in her bassinet, she's winning over her audience.

"You know something?" Sam whispers one night. "This is easily my favorite time. I could listen to her all night."

"And probably will," I add.

But Sam is right. The monkeys on horseback bring comfort and cheap entertainment. It's silence that jars us now, and has Sam ready to dial 911. "Send every car you have. My baby's stopped breathing."

"Evelyn's fine," I say, placing the phone back in its cradle. "Remember, honey. You've got to nap when baby naps."

Eventually, I heed that advice myself ... for all of a minute. But the sirens start up. Again. The old folks are under attack, and it's my hitch once more. I gather my weapons — the diaper and wipe — and charge into the fray.

Off with the old. Wipe, wax, and buff.

"Come on, little girl, you're clean now." I'm stumbling through the minefield, wet diaper in hand. "Won't you please stop crying?"

But the sirens don't quit.

An invisible cat rubs against my ankle, and I'm trying to recall just what it was I meant to do before calling it a day. In the back of my mind, I hear Sam saying, "Why not get it over with? You'll be sorry if you forget." Evelyn will not stop screaming. My arms feel numb, and suddenly I'm hit — a knee-buckling blast of toxic gas — knocked to the floor with both eyes burning. "The Genie's overflowing. It needs to be emptied." That's what Sam had urged me to do, back when my head was too infatuated with its pillow to care about anything else. "You said you'd do it hours ago."

Inches from my face, a bunched-up diaper plops onto the carpet. The room is growing dark. The horror! The horror! "Evelyn," I whisper in the direction of the changing table, "I did this for you. Don't ever forget that Daddy loved you." Then to the doorway: "If you can hear me, honey, call 911."

You don't really understand

human nature unless you

know why a child on a merry-

go-round will wave at his

parents every time around

– and why his parents will

always wave back.*

_____

BILL TAMMEUS

*Originally appeared in The Kansas City Star.

CHAPTER SIXTEEN

ALL'S WELL.

Sweat pools beneath a pressed white shirt. My jacket feels tight, as does my tie. I am standing before a judge, defending my work, family, plans for the future, and proficiency at changing diapers. But each new question seems easier than the last, and I'm slowly coming to understand that The Honorable Judge Charlotte Hanson favors adoption. She wants the child we've been raising for six months to be ours.

For ten minutes, Sam and I talk of decorating a nursery, paying our mortgage and taxes, and the importance of properly installing a car seat. When the hearing concludes, caseworker Dawn takes photos of Mom, Dad, and baby together in the courtroom. We pose with the judge, and with the relatives who took time from work to witness this milestone. Brother Mac beams as if he were the one who first suggested adoption.

One month later, we're sitting at our kitchen table, staring at a birth certificate. Evelyn is legally ours; the State of Colorado no longer sees us as foster parents. A brand new bottle of champagne waits in the fridge. And if this isn't a date we'll commemorate in future years – we already have a Homecoming

Day for that purpose – we will certainly mark it tonight.

Sam's also reviewing our very first progress report, written the weekend before to birth mother Laura. *The goat has Evelyn pinned to the barn again*, it begins.

Sam took over from there. *The past seven months have flown by so fast. Evelyn is inquisitive, strong, and quick to smile. She continues to amaze us.*

Two hours pass, and I am enjoying my champagne buzz. "Twinkle, Twinkle, Little Star" sounds good on CD, as does the Debussy that follows. I am feeding a baby that is legally mine, even if I may have recently promised a judge I would never drink champagne before attempting such feats. Rain falls gently outside her window. Baby is quiet, she's finished her bottle.

I notice we're rocking in time to the music. Two cats shoot past her door.

As the rain picks up, I'm pondering just how unrecognizable my life would be to the me I once knew. Sleepless and selfless, or pretty damn close, I seem to have changed in every respect. I have placed that life in the hands of another, which wouldn't be so intimidating were she not wearing a bib. As it is, she owns my future, and while I realize there's much less of this than used to be, it could still go on a while. I'm hoping she shows mercy.

Of course, I know there will be times when she tells me to pull out Dante's *Inferno* and choose a new home, and times when she calls sobbing on her thought-activated-lobe-implant-phone to say she totaled the police car her friends talked her into borrowing. But in between those adrenalin-charged moments, I want to hear three simple words ... "You're okay, Dad" ... even if they are followed by, "for an old guy."

She interrupts my thoughts with an overdue burp. "Nice one, girl. Excellent projection." Once again it's Baby First, and the thoughts I'm fielding are hopeful ones. It hits me I'm enjoying my life, and that the next several years are loaded with potential. I may even be feeling ambivalence toward an old enemy, the one sworn to kill me. Is it possible the passing of time, that consummate predator, has been hiding a good side? Can life still surprise me?

Other thoughts waft through the night air like notes in a lullaby. I want my daughter to achieve that rare balance between kindness and razor-sharp wit. I want her to be thoughtful, to learn from others, discover for herself, and ultimately share her wisdom with the rest of us. I want her to have fun, seasons of it, so that she's able to tell her friends, "The video they made for my birth mother didn't lie. They are fun parents. Even if they are in bed by nine."

There is something else, of course. I want her to love the old man, now and forever. "So what will it be, girl? To paraphrase a classic Lennon-McCartney lyric — paraphrase, because it must cost a diaperload of money to quote a Lennon-McCartney lyric — will you continue to require my presence and provide sustenance when I'm at an age between 63 and 65?"

She's smiling at me now, drooling at the edges, and somehow that's enough. She can have the keys to my car, safety deposit box, and heart. What do I care if she's trying to remove Hobbes' tail with a tiny clenched fist, or that Cousin Luke is still living in the basement two weeks after dropping by "for a few days to meet your angel"? So long as she keeps smiling. And gurgling. And squeezing my little finger. *Smile, baby, smile. The old man waited a long time to see this.*

It is a pleasant thing to

reflect upon, and furnishes

a complete answer to those

who contend for

the gradual degeneration of

the human species,

that every baby born into

the world is a finer one than

the last.

———————————

CHARLES DICKENS

AN EPILOGUE OF SORTS,

TEN YEARS ON.

I have seen into the future, but only by living it.

Ten years have passed since I first met Evelyn... eight since I visited my hometown, and went to an open house at brother Eddie's to hear someone give me shit, my hometown's primary source of employment, in the form of "He's fifty, and he's got a baby!"

This, if I am to trust a recent refresher in fifth-grade math, makes me fifty-eight, which means that when I stay up to watch the beginning of *Saturday Night Live*, I say one of two things upon seeing the host, either "He's looking old," or "Who is she?" We have new cats no longer so new, and a dog that chases them. We have one fish. Bubba outlived two others to take control of the tank and food supply. He isn't much smaller than the cats.

On that long-ago night we borrowed a bassinet from our good friends in Boulder, I was told, "You're not going to sleep for a while. We haven't since our first was born. But without kids, life would get boring." I have repeated these last words in my head many times, having long come to accept them as truth. Being a parent isn't all fun, but even with soccer tournaments and the Disney Channel, it rarely gets boring.

I have experienced so many great moments, like watching Evelyn take her first steps. And making up songs on guitar and violin with an inventive musician who tricked her father, yet again, into giving her a break from her assigned lessons. And finding myself in total agreement with a seven-year-old's critique of a novel we were reading together: "She's not like the Mary Poppins in the movie."

As it turns out, I was wise to entrust my future to that bib-wearing infant. My daughter has shown herself to be an excellent teacher, which made her the perfect teacher for a student like me who had so much to learn.

And what exactly was that?

Like parents of all ages, I learned I can take the urgent care visits, the washable paint spills that turn out to be permanent, and the occasional open rebellion. I learned I can bounce back after getting beat up by ten-year-olds who have too much energy before bedtime and need to release it by physically abusing old people. (She thinks she's wrestling.) "That's it, Dad! I'm taking you down!"

Like other adoptive parents, I have talked with my kid about adoption, exploring issues that will give Evelyn's life its own complexity and depth. From this, I learned that kids come up with pretty tough questions — most typically when they're supposed to be closing their eyes for the night. "So what you're asking, Evelyn, is, did I always know I wanted you specifically, and how could that be possible? Aren't you tired, sweetie? You've got to be tired. I know I'm too tired to consider the possibility that you and I might never have met in a universe slopped together through a series of random events. What if we talked in the morning?"

I do the best I can.

Luckily, as it turns out, my best is pretty damn good.

How else to explain my reaction when a baby vomited milk curdled in the oven of a flu-stricken stomach? Holding her out in front of me, I gently encouraged Evelyn to "Throw up on Daddy. No need to get it on the furniture."

And what of the Christmas morning I waited three hours for antibiotics in the only drug store open that day? Or my devoting four days to hand-painting and assembling a wooden dollhouse before grudgingly giving some mythical clown in a strange red suit all the credit for my labor? I know I get points for that first year of preschool, when every virus with bad intentions followed my daughter home. That's how I learned that sending a kid out into the world is like having the Europeans "discover" your continent.

There have been bigger surprises, not all clearly marked Good or Bad when they first inserted themselves into our lives. My mother provided the biggest of these when she moved west to make sure Evelyn knew damn well who Grandma was. Seven years later, we're easily into Mom for thirty grand in unbilled babysitting fees, kid game downloads, and Happy Meals.

Evelyn and Grandma are the closest of friends, as well as colluders and co-stars in Colorado's longest-running living-room-based improvisational theater. "We're playing school now, Grandma. You're the student." Though well into her eighties, Grandma is every bit the chauffeur, chef, and tutor I am. She forces me to admit I'm not too old to keep plugging away by showing reserves of energy that I hope are embedded somewhere in my genetic code. As for my own relations with Grandma, we're closer than we've been since I was ten. The move has been good for everyone.

The worst two surprises left nothing to ambivalence. Both came this past year, and both had to do with our being older parents. While Evelyn still loves the "strong Daddy" who lifts her off the ground with one arm, she came close to losing him, along with her mom. Sam took the first blow, when what felt like a pulled muscle turned out to be breast cancer, the very disease that took her mother's life. She learned this last fall, shortly after we hosted a Halloween party for five of Evelyn's friends. Upon receiving the diagnosis – Stage 2, detected early – Sam bristled at the thought of being defined as "someone with cancer." She didn't want to make pink a big part of her wardrobe.

Evelyn handled the initial news well. Although she turned white when asked, "Do you know what cancer is?" her color came back as she learned more. She seemed to accept we trusted our doctors and what they were saying. The next five months would be strange, but Mommy would get through this.

The following day, while riding in my car, Evelyn asked questions that were neither too shallow nor deep. "Mom really caught it early?" "The medicine will get rid of all the cancer?" She would get through this, too.

With Dad and Grandma working double shifts to keep our kid's life as kid-like as possible, Evelyn continued to have a good year at school. Dad took her shopping for clothes. Aunt Erin took Mom's place in a recital audience to hear Evelyn coax sweet, sonorous notes from her instrument of choice.

In grown-up world, our long winter got longer. The doc-tors' early optimism – minor surgery, a lumpectomy at most – gave way to the official diagnosis of Triple Negative cancer. "It's still Stage 2," the oncologist explained, "but the tumor is larger than we first thought. Triple Negative is a very aggressive cancer." More surgery was scheduled. This would be followed by sixteen weeks of intensive chemotherapy. Sam's hair would fall out. Every last strand.

She remained tough, making it through surgery and half of her chemo with surprisingly few complaints. Then, with February at its most frigid, the fever hit. One hundred and three... one hundred and four. Knowing that an infection could prove fatal if not treated promptly, we waited impatiently for the oncologist to return our calls. Hours passed. Sam felt queasy, then dizzy. When her fingertips turned purple, we raced to the nearest emergency room, where Sam was placed on oxygen. Technicians administered blood tests to detect infection. But as we were told, the results wouldn't be available for days, by which time the antibiotics either would – or wouldn't – have worked. Late that night, they sent us home to wait and see. Evelyn stayed with Grandma.

Short of sleep, and shorter still of ideas, I sat at my desk the following morning. Staring at my screen through eyes that had not slept for more than two hours at a time, I wished I could write something to make sense of our tenuous reality, enabling me to reclaim the illusion I had some control over life. But I had gone from being the optimist prone to remarking, "The prognosis could have been much worse," to being the guy who secretly wondered, "What aren't they telling us?" Slowly, I typed, Each time we think we've finally hit bottom, we learn it's only another pothole. There is always another, deeper bottom.

I heard Sam in the kitchen, and with some apprehension, went to see what she needed. My wife, by this time, had only two modes: complaining in bed about burning and aching, and coming downstairs to complain about the dishes in the sink. She couldn't comprehend that the dishes offered tangible proof that I had been keeping both Evelyn and her, to the extent it was possible, fed. I heated chicken soup. Sam tried to eat some.

184 · GEEZER DAD

Late that evening, after Evelyn had fallen asleep to the sound of Dad's voice reading *Freak the Mighty*, Sam's sister called to ask, "I know you just drove me to the airport a few days ago, but do I need to be there?" I told Erin no, saying there was little anyone could do, apart from washing the dishes I was finally washing.

Watching the water drain out of the sink, leaving a ring of fragile suds, I wondered how Evelyn was processing all that she was seeing. She had to know Mom was sicker than we had been expecting, but she also knew chemo could beat up its users pretty bad. For what may have been the first time, I pondered life as a widowed older dad. Beyond the shock and pain, would I be able to pull that off, and what kind of support network would I have? Would Evelyn and I stay in this house? Would we stay in Colorado, or move to the Midwest, taking Grandma with us, to be closer to Evelyn's younger cousins, the sons and daughters of my nieces and nephews? These questions brought guilt, but didn't seem out of place.

I heard footsteps behind me, too loud for a cat, too subtle for a dog. "Aren't you supposed to be asleep, Sweetie?" I asked.

"Is Mommy going to die?"

I knelt down on the kitchen's hardwood floor, not the best place for ageing knees. "I don't think so. It just takes her body longer to fight a virus or infection because it's already busy fighting the cancer. If you keep painting pictures and giving her hugs... not right now, we're going back to bed... Mommy should get better." I could hear the music from Evelyn's iPod, still playing upstairs. Grieg. *Notturno from Lyric Suite, Opus 54*. It's in a different playlist from Katie Perry and Taylor Swift, or for that matter, *Films about Ghosts* and *Yellow Submarine Songtrack*, two albums presumably missing from the collections of my daughter's less fortunate friends.

I offered to sit with her for a while. With little time wasted, she fell back asleep to *Pavane for a Dead Princess*, adapted for orchestra and played very slowly, which also made for one sleepy Dad. When I next opened my eyes, her clock read 4:35.

Two days later, the fever broke. The doctors called to say Sam had tested positive for infection, but that it must have been halted, given her recovery, before gaining a solid foothold. The following morning, standing before the toaster, Sam said weakly, "I know you did your best to keep things in order."

With two weeks lost, we restarted chemo. Friends and relatives lined up once more to display their incredible generosity and concern. Food appeared, already prepared, outside our front door. But this turned out to be problematic, at least for me. I was stressed, and depressed, and surrounded by protein-rich meals meant to keep my wife from losing weight. It wasn't a good combination.

Sam completed her full recovery in April. All test results read negative – the good negative – and we started planning for a vacation in early June. Together with Erin and other family members, we would rent a house on North Carolina's Outer Banks. Once there, Evelyn wouldn't be able to turn around without finding a cousin to play with. Sam and I would celebrate our renewed optimism by sharing an oceanfront room.

June came, and while preparing to take the dog for his last walk before Pet Camp, I told Sam I needed to call our doctor to review the blood pressure meds I'd been taking for two years. My readings had been slightly elevated, much like my weight. As soon as we returned from North Carolina, I would finally say goodbye to our long winter by addressing both problems.

"You're not going to call before we leave?" Sam said.

"Too many trip-imposed deadlines. And waiting two weeks isn't going to kill me." Kneeling by our front door, with an easily excited rescue Lab licking my face, I was now tying my shoes. This, I should be too embarrassed to admit, is one more thing I learned as a parent. When Evelyn was four, we caught an episode of *Sesame Street* in which Big Bird tied one of his freakishly huge shoes. The bird showed great meticulousness, and a series of extreme close-ups made it impossible to miss the slightest detail. I took a personal interest, as this had been my darkest secret since grade school: I did not know how to properly tie my shoes, having been the kid who daydreamed through countless tutorials, forcing him to later invent his own highly flawed system. There was one little twist I could never figure out, and all through my adult life, my shoes refused to stay tied for more than thirty minutes in one stretch. This slowed me down when racing through airports, hiking with friends, and running from bears encountered while hiking with friends. With my daughter sitting beside me, Big Bird changed all that. Big Bird taught me how to tie shoes, and I was a better man for this. The next bear would have trouble catching me.

Back on my feet, I fastened the dog's leash to his collar. "I promise to call my doctor as soon as we're back."

"I hope that means hours and not weeks," Sam said, displaying a depth of insight that comes only from decades of marriage. "Otherwise, your doctor won't be the only one unhappy with you."

The vacation started with two days to ourselves, during which time we explored the shores north of Cape Hatteras. Driving to our motel on a Thursday afternoon, we stopped to show Evelyn the Wright Brothers monument at Kitty Hawk. After climbing a pissant-by-Colorado-standards hill to reach that monument, an elderly couple took our photo. Then, Sam requested one of me standing alone in front of the word, "genius," excised from a longer inscription. When I tried telling the strangers, "She intends it to be ironic," I couldn't pull up a single word, not even the "to." In frustration, I stayed silent.

A minute later, I regained the ability to arrange words in sentences. I spoke the six words I had searched for in vain, though my joke had been lost to bad timing. Sam took more photos.

Walking down the hill, I told her what had happened, along with how strange and helpless I had felt. "You'd better drive," I added. But since she had not witnessed anything unusual, she blamed what I described on heat and exertion. I didn't point out that our climb had been unimpressive, or that the heat near the beach was hardly oppressive.

Two days later, heading for our final destination, I lost my ability to speak again. While driving across a long, arching bridge, I tried to show Evelyn a raised railroad drawbridge. Words like "rabbit," "sky," and "fishing" came out. It was late afternoon, just as it had been when I experienced the TIA.

Turning to face Sam in the front passenger seat, I struggled to let her know some invisible punch had knocked the English major out of me – again – and without using any of the words I was trying to summon, managed to convey the message. "Pull over," she instructed, and I cut across two lanes of traffic. I got out of the car, and recalling a Red Cross symbol I had seen, attempted to communicate we had passed a clinic or hospital only minutes before. Speaking slowly, and with great effort, I eventually inserted "clinic" between random words like "unless" and "doctor." I then tried telling Sam I must be having a stroke. I doubt this last word ever made its way out, but she already knew.

Within two minutes, we were facing Carteret Hospital's Emergency Room entrance. No sooner had Sam found a parking space than I charged out of the car and into the building to tell nurses I "cow climb tourniquet," or something that made as much sense.

"Sit down, Tom. Sit down," I heard my wife say as she took charge.

Then, I was lying in a bed in ICU, while my daughter, looking every bit as concerned as her mom and the nurses, stared at her strange, new dad. Unfamiliar with the workings of a stroke, I assumed it could only get worse. My life would slip slowly away, or worse, my family would fly home with an incoherent invalid for their one pricey souvenir. I would turn my daughter into a caretaker at ten years of age, voiding all my hopes for her future. Smug people would say, "They were too old to have kids."

When Aunt Erin showed up at the hospital to rescue Evelyn, by taking her to the beach house, one more face stared back with apprehension. I got one last, long hug from my daughter, and watching her walk through the door into the hallway, I realized I might be saying goodbye. For keeps. My heart hurt worse than my head.

Then, to everyone's surprise, not least of all my own, I began speaking in sentences. And what turned out to be a very localized stroke — three hits to the brain's left hemisphere where language is formed — showed itself to be in remission. By the time I took my first-ever ambulance ride to a much larger facility in Greenville, I was boring the paramedic with details meant to reassure my brain that it was working properly. My wig-wearing cancer-survivor wife followed in our rental car for all of ninety miles. It was midnight when we reached Pitt County Memorial Hospital.

I spent the next day touching my nose, telling curiously un-informed doctors what year it was, and getting inserted into every large machine the hospital owned. Showing no signs of physical impairment, I impressed the ICU staff with my resil-ience. One young guy even called from the hall: "You're awesome." I knew I would see my daughter again, and she would see the dad she remembered. The head neurologist promised to get us back to our vacation as early as the following morning, provided my signs stayed good – and I promised to avoid food that relied entirely on salt and fat for its taste, or basically everything served in North Carolina. I would also start taking new blood pressure pills, along with a daily baby aspirin "to keep the platelets slippery." My brain, he further explained, would construct efficient bypasses around each damaged section of neural highway. It would even recycle the three clots, making use of that material.

Late Monday morning, a nurse delivered my discharge papers. We were on our way to the beach – and Evelyn. When I walked back into the bright, humid air outside, I did so resolving to keep on moving, and for three months now, this is what I've been doing. My life continues, albeit with fewer food choices, and I remain more committed than ever before to survive another few decades. I will be there for my daughter.

This is an obligation that can't be annulled, only modified, even as loving child turns surly teen turns young adult fighting to define herself. Evelyn's old man will be the real thing then, no matter how passionately he pleads to be labeled by some other measure. It won't be enough to just be alive. I'll have to stay interesting and alert, refusing to prematurely burden a 25-year-old daughter with tales of hemorrhoids and color-coded pill dispensers. I won't get to be boring.

These are the choices I made – the choices my child made easier. Ten years into parenthood, I maintain it's all been worth it, without having to add an asterisk. And if the clock insists on ticking away, then I must keep ticking, too. When my birthday rolls around this fall, and Sam proudly announces, "I picked up your two favorites, New York Cheese Cake and Boston Cream

Pie," I will politely decline, saying, "Sorry, but no. I'm saving space for a second helping of broccoli." And when I buckle seconds later, muttering, "Well... maybe two small pieces won't do much damage," I will do so knowing it's a once-per-year transgression (twice if counting the cherry and pumpkin pie I will eat at Thanksgiving). But for 363 days each year, I'll be okay with the green stuff. And if I can't always make the choices I want, at least I'm making choices.

In this scenario, I can still go for walks around Harper Lake, encountering other walkers who look back at a stranger lost in thought, or a neighbor from down the street, or a writer whose second novel is somewhere in their house, or a guy who's getting a little bit older but doesn't let it slow him down. And I still get to meet a school bus each weekday at four, to watch Evelyn smile as she bounds off the last step, and looks up to see the part of me that matters most. Dad. Daddy. Old Dad.

I love you, kid. I love you so much I want you to thrive in my absence, to keep treasuring life when I'm no longer part of it. But I also plan to put this off as long as possible, refusing to write myself out of the story before I have moved furniture into your first apartments, masterminded the mysterious disappearance of an unsuitable boyfriend or two, and sent you countless long-distance emails I know you won't actually read.

You have already given me more than I ever needed... just this morning, in fact, when you crashed into me with open arms, and loudly declared, "I love my daddy."

And what of that magical, outside-of-time hug you had waiting for me when I returned to our vacation in North Carolina? That had to be the best medical care anyone ever received. For however long it lasted, your dad felt truly awesome.

It's hard to believe ten years have passed. This, after all, is a lifetime to one of us. As for the old man, I'm a thousand years older than when Mom and I first talked about having a child, yet younger in so many ways, these lying gray hairs to the contrary. I have never known ten better years, packed as they were with moments I wanted to snatch from time's grip, refusing to let them pass. On so many occasions, I felt like I was listening to great music, thinking nothing could surpass the melody and richness of texture, only to find the next movement equally satisfying, perhaps even more so because it caught me off guard.

Just as one dad's epilogue is his daughter's prologue, life must keep changing, repeatedly, relentlessly. Yet, some of the changes can truly amaze. Having taken the long way to reach this point, I see no need to rush the last part of my journey, especially if you keep traveling with me. Let's savor each change, taking our time, however it ends up being measured, in years or in decades. Let's seize the adventure coming our way.

In the meantime, we've got homework to finish and critters to feed. And should we stop to debate how many times one-eighth goes into four, I promise we will sort it out. That's what erasers are for – hugs, too. If you learn nothing else from your old dad, apart of course from all this surprisingly advanced math, never forget it's worth getting things right, no matter how much patience and persistence are required, whether you're struggling to master a new piece on violin, or trying to reach that place you were always meant to occupy. I know this from experience – you could say, I learned it the long way – and should you need substantiation, then I have a story to tell you someday.

ABOUT TOM LAMARR

The median age for becoming a parent has climbed, and Tom LaMarr is the reason. The *Geezer Dad* author was nearly 48 when he met his daughter, which makes him even older now.

He is also the author of two acclaimed novels. *October Revolution*, hailed by three separate publications as "a remarkable first novel," prompted *Catch-22* author Joseph Heller to write, "Got back home and read your novel with much ease, excitement, and pleasure. I found it 'a lighthearted, dandy satire with a humorous plot and a variety of deft pops at many deserving targets.' And you can quote me."

Hallelujah City also received favorable reviews, including this from *Publishers Weekly*: "LaMarr has created a hectic, full-bodied account of a troubled young lady enmeshed in a bizarre religious cult... The plot is stocked with enough tension to hook readers until the chaotic, fiery climax." *The Boulder Camera* noted, "*Hallelujah City*, like LaMarr's debut novel, is a fast and funny read. Humor isn't easy to pull off, but LaMarr does it effortlessly... Yet *Hallelujah City* is a melancholy novel, a meditation on mistakes that can never really be unmade.

That tension, between laughter and tears, makes it deeper and more complex than many a *New York Times* bestseller."

After growing up on a bluff overlooking the Mississippi River in Dubuque, Iowa, Tom lived and worked in Council Bluffs and Des Moines, then Jacksonville, Florida (where he met his wife), and the District of Columbia. He studied at the University of Iowa Fiction Writers Workshop, and has called Colorado home for more than two decades.

Photo by Allie J.

ACKNOWLEDGEMENTS

It took a village to write this book. Love and thanks to my daughter and wife for giving me a gift far more valuable than any story on paper, while still giving me a pretty good story. Thanks, too, to the real-life counterparts of Dawn, Ellen, Jane, and others far too wise, fair, and kind to ever consider lawsuits.

As for helping with the actual paperwork, I am greatly indebted to Timothy Hillmer, Robert (*"I'm going in"*) McBrearty, Bill Jones, Mark Lamprey, Kat LaMons, Trish Diggins, Chet Hampson, Lucia Fiori, Mark Kjeldgaard, Robert Ebisch, Jane Dystel, Sandra Bond, Karen Palmer, Juliet Wittman, Robert Byrne, and Colleen Johnson.

Finally, I must acknowledge the important people in my life who are about to find themselves marginally fictionalized. In bringing a few supporting characters to life, I created composites of multiple friends and family members, a trick that allowed me to include many viewpoints without introducing 200 characters, and making you try to remember their names. My "brother in Denver" is one such character, and thus bears only a slight resemblance to my brilliant, funny, married brother in Denver. All of which brings me to the one truth I refused to tamper with in writing this book: I have the best family and friends available in this world, and it's hard to imagine this story without them.

Additional copies of this book may be purchased through most online book retailers and by request through major and independent bookstores.

To purchase this book for your bookstore, library, or in bulk, please contact the publisher at www.marcinsonpress.com.

MARCINSON PRESS